ASPEN PUBLISH

Friedmans
Practice Series

Civil Procedure

Edited by

Professor Joel Wm. Friedman

Tulane University Law School
Jack M. Gordon Professor of Procedural Law & Jurisdiction

Wolters Kluwer
Law & Business

AUSTIN   BOSTON   CHICAGO   NEW YORK   THE NETHERLANDS

To contact Customer Care, e-mail customer.care@aspenpublishers.com, call 1-800-234-1660, fax 1-800-901-9075, or mail correspondence to:

Aspen Publishers
Attn: Order Department
PO Box 990
Frederick, MD 21705

Printed in the United States of America.

1 2 3 4 5 6 7 8 9 0

ISBN 978-0-7355-8619-2

About Wolters Kluwer Law & Business

Wolters Kluwer Law & Business is a leading provider of research information and workflow solutions in key specialty areas. The strengths of the individual brands of Aspen Publishers, CCH, Kluwer Law International and Loislaw are aligned within Wolters Kluwer Law & Business to provide comprehensive, in-depth solutions and expert-authored content for the legal, professional and education markets.

CCH was founded in 1913 and has served more than four generations of business professionals and their clients. The CCH products in the Wolters Kluwer Law & Business group are highly regarded electronic and print resources for legal, securities, antitrust and trade regulation, government contracting, banking, pension, payroll, employment and labor, and healthcare reimbursement and compliance professionals.

Aspen Publishers is a leading information provider for attorneys, business professionals and law students. Written by preeminent authorities, Aspen products offer analytical and practical information in a range of specialty practice areas from securities law and intellectual property to mergers and acquisitions and pension/benefits. Aspen's trusted legal education resources provide professors and students with high-quality, up-to-date and effective resources for successful instruction and study in all areas of the law.

Kluwer Law International supplies the global business community with comprehensive English-language international legal information. Legal practitioners, corporate counsel and business executives around the world rely on the Kluwer Law International journals, loose-leafs, books and electronic products for authoritative information in many areas of international legal practice.

Loislaw is a premier provider of digitized legal content to small law firm practitioners of various specializations. Loislaw provides attorneys with the ability to quickly and efficiently find the necessary legal information they need, when and where they need it, by facilitating access to primary law as well as state-specific law, records, forms and treatises.

Wolters Kluwer Law & Business, a unit of Wolters Kluwer, is headquartered in New York and Riverwoods, Illinois. Wolters Kluwer is a leading multinational publisher and information services company.

About the Editor

Joel Wm. Friedman
Tulane Law School
Jack M. Gordon Professor of Procedural Law & Jurisdiction,
  Director of Technology
BS, 1972, Cornell University; JD, 1975, Yale University

Professor Joel Wm. Friedman, the Jack M. Gordon Professor of Procedural Law & Jurisdiction at Tulane Law School, is the lead author of two highly regarded casebooks — The Law of Civil Procedure: Cases and Materials (published by Thomson/West) and The Law of Employment Discrimination (published by Foundation Press). His many law review articles have been published in, among others, the Cornell, Texas, Iowa, Tulane, Vanderbilt, and Washington & Lee Law Reviews.

Professor Friedman is an expert in computer-assisted legal instruction who has lectured throughout the country on how law schools can integrate developing technologies into legal education. He is a past recipient of the Felix Frankfurter Teaching Award and the Sumpter Marks Award for Scholarly Achievement.

Contents

CIVIL PROCEDURE
ESSAY EXAMINATION
QUESTIONS

CIVIL PROCEDURE ESSAY EXAM #1

Bio Dream, Inc. (BDI), a corporation incorporated under the laws of Delaware, specializes in the development and manufacture of pharmaceutical products. Over the past few years, it has invested heavily in genetic engineering and, on January 5, 2003, revealed to the world that the scientists in its laboratory in San Jose, California, had engineered a designer drug named Mindex that could slow down the development of Alzheimer's Disease. The press release, issued through its corporate headquarters in Los Angeles, California, also announced that BDI had entered into a partnership with Ace Pharmaceutical Enterprises (APE), the nation's second largest pharmaceutical distributor, in which APE would be the exclusive worldwide distributor of Mindex. APE, a corporation incorporated under New York law, agreed to ship all Mindex from its central warehouse in Chicago to drugstores and other retail outlets throughout the United States and Canada.

On March 16, 2008, Jeremy Steel purchased a one-year's supply of Mindex from Stop & Shop, a neighborhood drugstore in his hometown of Miami, Florida. He took the pill once a day without fail over the next six months, including a two-week period from September 2-15, 2008, when he and his wife were on holiday in Las Vegas, Nevada. Unfortunately for the Steels, Jeremy became gravely ill during that vacation and, upon examination at the Lotta Hope Hospital in Las Vegas, was informed by an internist that he had contracted a rare and incurable liver disease as a side effect of taking Mindex. Too sick to be moved, Jeremy remained in a Las Vegas hospital until his untimely demise on December 25, 2008.

After returning to her home in Miami, Jeremy's wife, Hermione, contacted an attorney who recommended that she bring a wrongful death tort action against BDI, APE, and Stop & Shop seeking $15 million in compensatory and punitive damages against each defendant as a result of their part in the manufacture, inspection, distribution, and sale of Mindex. But based on the attorney's indication that Nevada tort law provided the best likelihood of recovery on the claims, Hermione filed this action against BDI, APE, and Stop & Shop in the federal district court for the District of Nevada located in Las Vegas. In addition to her wrongful death claims, Hermione's complaint included a claim that BDI had violated the terms of the federal Food and Drug Act by not conducting a sufficiently lengthy longitudinal study of the drug's effects prior to putting Mindex on the market.

After accepting service, each of the defendants filed an answer that contained a motion to dismiss the claims against them. In addition, BDI asserted two claims against Dr. Lou Johnson, inventor of Mindex. Its first claim sought indemnity against any judgment recovered against it on the ground that Johnson, a California citizen, was the inventor of Mindex and therefore was ultimately responsible for its failures. Its second claim sought recovery of moneys paid to Johnson as reimbursement for an alleged business trip (associated with his research on another drug) that he had fraudulently submitted in October 2003.

The Nevada legislature has enacted the following statute:

> The courts of this state shall have personal jurisdiction over a person, corporation, or other entity, who, in person or through an agent:
> (1) commits a tortious act within the state;
> (2) transacts business within the state;
> (3) owns property within the state; or
> (4) is personally served within the state.

QUESTION #1 (70%)

You are the law clerk for the judge to whose docket this case has been assigned. Draft a memorandum to the judge discussing all possibly relevant bases for dismissing any or all of the claims in this lawsuit. Include in your memorandum all of the arguments that could be made in support of and in opposition to the dismissal of these claims as well as your recommendation as to whether or not each claim should be dismissed.

QUESTION #2 (15%)

Assume that Hermione had sued only BDI and Stop & Shop and that she had filed the suit in state court in Las Vegas. The attorneys for BDI and Stop & Shop removed the case. How should the court rule on the plaintiff's timely motion to remand?

QUESTION #3 (15%)

Assume that all jurisdictional objections were overruled and that Hermione prevailed on the merits against BDI in federal court in Nevada. After hearing of Hermione's victory, Justine Long, an Iowa citizen, brought suit against BDI in state court in Iowa. In its answer, BDI denied all of Justine's allegations and disclaimed any liability for consequences which, it maintained, could not be linked to Mindex. In response, Justine filed a motion with the court asking that it strike these defenses from the answer and thereby limit trial to the issue of damages. How should the court rule on this motion?

CIVIL PROCEDURE ESSAY EXAM #2

On March 1, 2007, Pat Green, an entrepreneur who operates a mail order business out of her home in Pittsburgh, purchased 1,000 shares of stock in High Flier, Inc. (HFI) at $55 per share after reading its prospectus at the local office of a stock brokerage firm. On that same day, Leslie Arrow, an artist living in Taos, New Mexico, purchased 50 shares of HFI at that same price after reading an article about HFI in the local newspaper. HFI is a publicly held technology company whose stock is listed on the NASDAQ exchange, has shareholders residing in all 50 states, and which is incorporated under the laws of Delaware. It is headquartered in the heart of "Silicon Valley"—San Jose, California. It also maintains regional satellite offices in Denver, Houston, Chicago, and Boston, where it markets and services its products through a staff of ten employees at each satellite location. For the past 12 years, as required by the federal Securities Act, HFI submitted annual earnings reports to the Securities and Exchange Commission (SEC) with the understanding that these reports would be made available to the general public. In each of those 12 annual reports, HFI reported a 25% increase in net profits from the preceding year. These reports were prepared for HFI by Dewey, Cheatam & Howe, Inc. (DCH), an independent accounting firm that also conducted HFI's annual audit. DCH is incorporated under the laws of Pennsylvania. It maintains large offices in Los Angeles, San Francisco, and San Diego, and employs a local representative in New York and Chicago.

In January 2008, Paul Snerdley, the president of HFI, who authorized the submission of HFI's annual reports to the SEC, used half of the $25 million that he had obtained by cashing in some of his shares of HFI to purchase a luxurious mansion in Malibu, California. He resides there with his wife, daughter, $10 million art collection, and four Rolls Royces when he is not vacationing at one of his homes in Paris, Bermuda, Hawaii, or Cape Cod.

In response to an anonymous tip received on February 1, 2008, the SEC conducted an investigation into HFI's finances and discovered that the company, through its annual audits, grossly misrepresented its financial position from 2000-2008. As a result, the SEC instructed NASDAQ to halt trading on HFI stock as of April 15, 2008. As news of the SEC investigation became public, HFI investors scrambled to cut their losses. By the time Pat and Leslie sold their shares on April 1, 2008, the per share price of HFI stock had dropped to $1.50. When, two weeks thereafter, the SEC decision was announced, Pat and Leslie contacted an attorney to advise them of their possible rights against HFI, DCH, and the leadership of both of these entities.

On January 2, 2009, Pat and Leslie filed an action in federal district court in Santa Fe, New Mexico, against HFI, DCH, and Paul Snerdley. In that lawsuit, Pat and Leslie each brought a claim for declaratory relief against HFI seeking a declaration that by filing false and misleading representations in its annual reports to the SEC the company violated the terms of the federal Securities and Exchange Act of 1934.

Pat and Leslie each also asserted a fraud-based state law tort claim seeking $50,000 in compensatory damages against each defendant. HFI, in turn, filed a claim for indemnity against DCH as well as a breach of contract claim seeking a refund of the $200,000 in accounting fees it had paid to DCH over the past 12 years. DCH filed an indemnity claim against Susan Goff, its senior accountant responsible for the HFI account. Finally, Snerdley filed a defamation claim against both Pat and Leslie alleging that they brought their claims in bad faith and that the instigation of this litigation had severely damaged his reputation, for which he sought $65,000 in damages.

The New Mexico legislature has enacted the following statute:

> The courts of this state shall have personal jurisdiction over a person, corporation, or other entity, who, in person or through an agent:
> (1) commits a tortious act within the state;
> (2) transacts business within the state;
> (3) owns property within the state; or
> (4) is personally served within the state.

QUESTION #1 (80%)

You are the law clerk for the judge to whose docket this case has been assigned. Assuming that there has been no waiver of any such objection, draft a memorandum to the judge discussing all possibly relevant bases for dismissing any or all of the claims in this lawsuit. Include in your memorandum all of the arguments that could be made in support of and in opposition to the dismissal of these claims as well as your recommendation as to whether or not each claim should be dismissed.

QUESTION #2 (15%)

Assume all of the facts mentioned above except that the lawsuit was filed in a state court in Santa Fe. The attorneys for HFI, DCH, and Snerdley removed the case. How should the court rule on the plaintiffs' motion to remand?

QUESTION #3 (5%)

After a trial in the case discussed above, the jury issued a verdict in favor of the defendants on all counts. Thereafter, the SEC brought an action against HFI and DCH alleging that their participation in the preparation of false and misleading statements in the annual reports violated the terms of the Securities and Exchange Act of 1934, for which the SEC sought $25 million in punitive damages. Your clients, HFI and DCH, want to bring a *nonjurisdictional* motion to dismiss this claim on grounds other than failure to state a claim upon which relief can be granted. Draft a memo explaining why you believe that such an effort would or would not be successful.

> ## CIVIL PROCEDURE ESSAY EXAM #3

Diamond Programs, Inc., entered into a contract on January 3, 2008, with Humanity Providers, Inc., under which Diamond agreed to manage and operate a hospice program located at Humanity's elderly care facility in Cleveland, Ohio. The contract further provided that Diamond would provide, train, and manage all employees working in the hospice, that all of these employees would be Ohio citizens, and that the hospice would serve only patients who are Ohio citizens. Diamond is incorporated under the laws of Delaware. Although it manages and operates other hospice facilities in New York and Connecticut, the Humanity hospice is Diamond's only operation in Ohio. All of Diamond's operations, including the Humanity hospice in Cleveland, are overseen by Diamond executives and supervisory personnel operating out of an office located in Indianapolis, Indiana. Humanity Providers is incorporated under the laws of Ohio and operates a range of health-related facilities throughout Ohio. Its headquarters, which includes all of its executive offices, is located in Cleveland. On December 1, 2008, Diamond filed an action against Humanity in the federal district court for the District of Indiana. The complaint alleged that Humanity failed to make its contractually required monthly payments to Diamond and sought damages in the amount of $1 million.

The negotiation of the agreement between the parties was conducted through an exchange of email and fax transmissions between the vice president of Administration for Diamond and the president of Humanity. The final agreement was signed by each of these individuals on behalf of their respective employer. On three different occasions, Diamond supervisors telephoned employees at the Humanity hospice with instructions on how to perform various tasks. In one of these situations, the problem was resolved only when the involved hospice employee met with her supervisors at Diamond's executive offices.

Jack Hammer, a citizen of Ohio, works at the Humanity hospice in Cleveland. He filed two claims against Humanity as part of the suit brought by Diamond against Humanity in the federal court in Indianapolis. In his first cause of action, Jack alleged that he was forced to work in an unsafe environment in violation of the Federal Occupational Safety and Health Act and sought damages in the amount of $50,000. He also brought a claim alleging that Humanity had breached his employment contract by failing to pay his wages (amounting to $25,000) since April 1, 2008.

After receiving a copy of the Diamond and Hammer complaints, Humanity filed a motion to dismiss the complaints, an answer denying all of the allegations contained in the complaints, and two additional claims. The first of these claims was against BancOhio, a bank organized under the laws of Ohio with its one and only branch in Cleveland and in which Humanity maintained a checking account. In this claim, Humanity asserted that if Diamond and Hammer never received their respective payments, it was caused by BancOhio's negligent failure to process checks and not by Humanity's failure to write the checks to these two payees. Humanity sought damages against the bank in the amount of $150,000 for damage to its reputation as well as indemnity for the claims brought against it by Hammer and Diamond. Humanity's second claim was against Diamond, alleging that its negligent supervision of the hospice workers in Cleveland resulted in inferior service provided to the hospice patients, which, in turn, injured Humanity's reputation in the business and health care communities, for which it sought damages in the amount of $50,000.

The Indiana and Ohio legislatures have enacted the following statute:

> The courts of this state shall have personal jurisdiction over a person, corporation, or other entity, who, in person or through an agent:
> (1) commits a tortious act within the state;
> (2) transacts business within the state;
> (3) owns property within the state; or
> (4) is personally served within the state.

QUESTION #1 (70%)

You are the law clerk for the judge to whose docket this case has been assigned. Draft a memorandum to the judge discussing all possibly relevant bases for dismissing any or all of the claims in this lawsuit. Include in your memorandum all of the arguments that could be made in support of and in opposition to the dismissal of these claims as well as your recommendation as to whether or not each claim should be dismissed.

QUESTION #2 (15%)

Assume that Diamond and Hammer had brought their lawsuit against Humanity in a state trial court in Indianapolis. You are the attorney for Humanity and upon receiving a copy of the complaint, your client instructed you to do whatever it took to have this case heard in the federal district court in Cleveland. Discuss the mechanisms you would use to accomplish that result, and explain whether or not you would be successful in that effort.

QUESTION #3 (15%)

Assume again that the Diamond/Hammer lawsuit against Humanity was filed in state court, but that Humanity did not assert, in that proceeding, any claim against BancOhio. Rather, it contested the merits and lost. Humanity subsequently filed a separate suit against BancOhio seeking indemnity and won. It then filed another suit against BancOhio seeking the $50,000 in damages to its reputation in the business and health care communities. In this latter action, Humanity filed a motion with the court asking it to preclude BancOhio from litigating the issue of its negligent failure to process checks. BancOhio, in turn, filed a motion to dismiss the complaint on nonjurisdictional/non-venue grounds. How should the court rule on each of these motions?

CIVIL PROCEDURE ESSAY EXAM #4

The Noise (Noise) is a new wave musical group composed of five musicians, all of whom were born and raised, and continue to live, in Los Angeles, California. Noise recorded its first CD, "Beautiful Music," in a recording studio in New York City on January 1, 2008. The recording was distributed by Capitol Records, Inc., pursuant to a contract giving Capitol exclusive rights to produce, market, and distribute all of Noise's recordings from 1999 until 2019. Capitol is incorporated under Delaware law and has its corporate headquarters, production, and distribution facilities in Los Angeles, California. Capitol recordings are sold in music stores throughout the country. Capitol generates $35 million in annual sales of its recordings, with 20% of all sales occurring in California and 25% of all sales occurring in New York.

In order to provide this local band (they have never performed outside of the southern California area) with some national visibility and thereby promote CD sales, the band's manager chose to aggressively market Noise over the Internet. To that end, he created a web page at www.thenoise.com where fans and other interested consumers could learn more about the band members and sample short excerpts from each of the songs on the new CD. On the other hand, the band was anxious to protect their stream of royalty payments by preventing individuals from distributing pirated versions of the CD or otherwise freely distributing electronic versions of their music.

Iggy Poop, a 16-year-old computer devotee from San Diego, California, was one of Noise's biggest fans. Iggy purchased a copy of the "Beautiful Music" CD on the day that it was released and immediately converted all of the individual selections on the CD to a digital (mp3) format on his computer. He then joined a file-sharing network that allowed all network participants to access and retrieve (i.e., download to their computers' hard drives), at no charge, mp3 files contained on the hard drives of all other network participants. This network was created and is maintained by Nerdster, Inc., a Delaware-incorporated business with its headquarters located in San Francisco, California. Nerdster has over 3 million users, including individuals from each of the 50 states within the United States. Within a month after joining Nerdster, Iggy had downloaded 150 songs via Nerdster. In addition, since Iggy's computer was connected to this Nerdster network, over 500 individuals from around the country retrieved the copy of "Beautiful Music" that was located on his computer through the Nerdster network.

In an attempt to discourage Iggy and everyone else from "stealing" their music, four of the five members (Jay Cool, the band's lead singer and most popular member, chose not to join in this action) of Noise brought a civil action in the federal district court in New York City (S.D.N.Y.) in which they alleged that Iggy had violated the terms of the U.S. Copyright Act. Each of these band members also brought a separate claim for tortious interference with contractual relations against Iggy. The complaints sought $50,000 in lost income damages in connection with each claim. Each of these four band members also brought a $250,000 breach of contract claim against Capitol, alleging that Capitol did not exercise its best efforts to promote the "Beautiful Music" CD.

After receiving a copy of the complaint, Iggy filed two claims in that action against Nerdster. The first claim sought indemnification for any liability that Iggy might be adjudged to have vis-à-vis the plaintiffs. The second claim alleged that the software negligently developed by Nerdster that all users had to load onto their computers in order to gain access to Nerdster's file-sharing capabilities had destroyed Iggy's computer, for which Iggy sought $25,000 in damages. Additionally, Iggy filed a claim against Capitol, alleging that its pricing policies violated the federal antitrust laws.

The New York legislature has enacted the following statute:

> The courts of this state shall have personal jurisdiction over a person, corporation, or other entity, who, in person or through an agent:
> (1) commits a tortious act within the state;
> (2) transacts business within the state;
> (3) owns property within the state; or
> (4) is personally served within the state.

QUESTION #1 (80%)

You are the law clerk for the judge to whose docket this case has been assigned. Draft a memorandum to the judge discussing all possibly relevant bases for dismissing any or all of the claims in this lawsuit. Include in your memorandum all of the arguments that could be made in support of and in opposition to the dismissal of these claims as well as your recommendation as to whether or not each claim should be dismissed.

QUESTION #2 (10%)

Assume all of the facts mentioned above except that the lawsuit was filed in a state trial court in New York City. The attorneys for Capitol and Iggy would like this case to be tried by a federal judge in New York City. Discuss the mechanisms they would employ to accomplish that result, and explain whether or not this effort will succeed.

QUESTION #3 (10%)

(a) Assume that the case mentioned above was filed in federal district court in New York and that the case went to trial on all the claims. After the trial court issued a judgment in favor of Iggy, Iggy filed a separate tort action against the members of Noise alleging that their institution of the lawsuit against him damaged his reputation and caused him to suffer severe emotional pain and suffering, for which he sought damages in the amount of $400,000. Discuss any argument that could be made in support of and in opposition to a nonjurisdictional/non–venue-based motion to dismiss this claim.

(b) Assume that the case was filed in federal district court in New York and went to trial on all claims. Also assume that the trial court ruled that Iggy had not violated the copyright laws in distributing his version of "Beautiful Music." One month after that judgment was rendered, Jay Cool filed an action in federal district court in Los Angeles against Iggy. His complaint alleges that Iggy violated the U.S. Copyright Act by making the music freely available through Nerdster and, because he received the lion's share of the group's royalties, sought damages in the amount of $500,000. Iggy filed a motion with the court asking it to refuse to litigate whether he violated the U.S. Copyright Act. How should the court rule on this motion?

CIVIL PROCEDURE ESSAY EXAM #5

On January 1, 2008, a rock/rap artist called "Bad Boy" (BB) released his first recording. Many of the selections on that CD contained graphic and violent lyrics, including one song that glorified the activities of an urban gang, all of whose members have been convicted of killing three police officers in Detroit. The CD received a lot of publicity and became a nationwide bestseller in its category. To promote sales, Bad Boy undertook a nationwide tour, in which he performed in 20 cities across the country.

BB is a 20-year-old male who was born and raised in Philadelphia. Prior to signing a long-term recording contract with MCI Records, Inc. (MCI), on December 1, 2006, BB had never been outside of Pennsylvania. His concert tour took him to, among other locations, New York, Los Angeles, Dallas, Houston, and New Orleans. BB performed a single concert in each city. In every instance, BB arrived the night before the scheduled concert and left the morning after that concert. MCI is incorporated under the laws of Delaware and has all of its corporate offices and recording studios in Los Angeles, California.

On November 1, 2008, two members of a gang in New Orleans were charged with murdering two police officers during an alleged drug bust. The spouses of both of the two officers brought one lawsuit in which they asserted a tort claim for damages against BB in the U.S. District Court for the Eastern District of Louisiana (in New Orleans) alleging that the lyrics in BB's song were a proximate cause of the death of their spouses because those lyrics encouraged the gang members to use violence against police officers. Each spouse is a lifelong resident of New Orleans and is seeking $1 million against BB. In that same lawsuit, each spouse also asserted a $1 million tort claim against MCI, claiming that by producing, recording, and distributing the CD, this defendant also was responsible for the death of the police officers. In their complaint, the plaintiffs note that the lyrics of each of BB's songs were available on MCI's web page, as was the opportunity to purchase the CD with the use of a credit card. The complaint also states a $50,000 tort claim against Tom's Music, a Los Angeles, California music store that sold the new BB CD. In this cause of action, a tort claim for damages, the plaintiffs allege not only that the store's promotion of the CD contributed to the environment that encouraged the gang members' violent conduct, but that the free speech provision of the First Amendment of the U.S. Constitution does not apply to, and thereby does not immunize from liability, Tom's decision to sell the offending CD.

After receiving a copy of the complaint, MCI filed a motion to dismiss the complaint as well as an answer and two claims against Joe Brown, the songwriter who wrote all the lyrics to all of the songs on the BB CD. In the first claim, MCI seeks indemnity from Brown on the ground that it was his lyrics, rather than its activities, which are to blame, if at all, for the death of the two police officers. The second claim is a breach of contract claim seeking $25,000 in damages for Brown's failure to provide the lyrics to another CD in a timely manner. Joe Brown is a citizen of California. Finally, MCI also filed a breach of contract claim against Tom's

Music, claiming that Tom's had not paid for a shipment of 1,500 CDs, including 300 copies of the CD by BB. In connection with this claim, MCI sought damages in the amount of $50,000.

The Louisiana legislature has enacted the following statute:

> The courts of this state shall have personal jurisdiction over a person, corporation, or other entity, who, in person or through an agent:
> (1) commits a tortious act within the state;
> (2) transacts business within the state;
> (3) owns property within the state; or
> (4) is personally served within the state.

QUESTION #1 (80%)

You are the law clerk for the judge to whose docket this case has been assigned. Draft a memorandum to the judge discussing all possibly relevant bases for dismissing any or all of the claims in this lawsuit. Include in your memorandum all of the arguments that could be made in support of and in opposition to the dismissal of these claims as well as your recommendation as to whether or not each claim should be dismissed.

QUESTION #2 (20%)

(a) Assume that all of the motions discussed in your answer to Question #1 are denied and that the jury found in favor of all of the defendants against the plaintiff spouses. Subsequently, BB filed a defamation action in a state trial court in New Orleans against the spouses of the two deceased police officers claiming that the public statements the spouses made against him during the course of their lawsuit damaged his reputation and that they intentionally caused him emotional and mental distress. BB sought $50,000 in damages on the defamation claim and $65,000 on the intentional infliction of emotional distress claim. The defendants have come to you for advice on whether there is any way, other than challenging jurisdiction or venue, to have the complaint dismissed against them. Discuss the arguments that could be asserted in support of and in opposition to such an effort and provide your assessment of the likely result.

(b) Assume that the court decides not to dismiss the complaint described in part (a) of this question. Also assume that in the spouses' lawsuit against BB, the jury, in response to a series of interrogatories, found that the damage suffered by the spouses amounted to $1.5 million, but that BB's recording was not a cause of the police officer's death. Assume further that the children of the two deceased police officers now file a tort claim for wrongful death against BB, alleging, as their parents did, that BB's CD contributed to the death of their parents. The children have filed a motion asking the court to preclude litigation on the issue of damages and BB has filed a motion asking the court to preclude litigation on the issue of causation. Describe fully how the court should rule on each of these motions.

CIVIL PROCEDURE ESSAY EXAM #6

Max Emillion had been living in his home on the banks of a bayou outside of Ville Platte, Louisiana for more than 20 years when the house was destroyed by a massive flood in the summer of 2007. The home was repaired and renovated in January 2008 by Cajun Builders, Inc. (CBI), a Delaware-incorporated corporation whose only office is in Lafayette, Louisiana. Although the president and chief operating officer of CBI, Paula Boudreaux, had moved permanently from Lafayette to Beverly Hills, California, back in 2005, she continued to serve as president and CEO of CBI. CBI is a general contractor that builds homes throughout western Louisiana and eastern Texas. Emillion had purchased a homeowner's insurance policy with Everystate Insurance Co. (EIC), a Delaware-incorporated insurance firm headquartered in Hartford, Connecticut. EIC insures homes located in every state in the United States. Its policies are sold by self-employed, independent insurance agents who offer their customers a range of policies from a variety of insurers, including Everystate. EIC also operates a web page that has general information on the types of policies that the company offers and directs interested individuals to contact their local independent insurance agent for additional information on specific EIC policies.

After the flood, Emillion submitted a claim with EIC, which the company denied on the ground that his homeowner's policy only covered wind damage and that the waters from the flood were the sole cause of the destruction of Emillion's home. It cost Emillion $250,000 to repair the damage to his home. On August 1, 2008, Emillion brought suit in federal district court for the Western District of Louisiana, located in Lafayette. His complaint contained the following:

(1) a claim against CBI alleging that its repairs to his flood-ravaged home did not meet standards for repair of flood-destroyed property contained in the federal Hurricane and Flood Restoration and Prevention Act of 2005, for which he sought damages in the amount of $250,000;

(2) a claim against CBI alleging that it had negligently repaired his home, for which he sought damages in the amount of $250,000;

(3) a claim against EIC alleging that its decision to deny his insurance claim violated the terms of his insurance contract, for which he sought damages in the amount of $250,000;

(4) a claim against Boudreaux alleging that Boudreaux had negligently failed to check the references of the subcontractor that she, on behalf of CBI, had hired to repair the windows in Emillion's home, for which Emillion sought damages in the amount of $58,000.

Within a month after receiving personal service, CBI, EIC, and Boudreaux filed answers that contained motions to dismiss all claims and parties. In addition, CBI filed an indemnity claim against Boudreaux alleging that as company president she was personally liable for all damages recovered against the company. It also filed a breach of contract claim against Boudreaux seeking recovery of the $35,000 monthly salary it had paid her for the months of June and July of 2008. EIC filed a $100,000 claim against Alexa Erich, an independent life insurance agent from New Haven, Connecticut, alleging that Alexa had fraudulently submitted requests for payment of finder's fees on 50 insurance contracts, none of which she actually sold.

The Louisiana legislature has enacted the following statute:

> The courts of this state shall have personal jurisdiction over a nonresident person, corporation, or other entity, who, in person or through an agent:
> (1) causes tortious injury within the state;
> (2) transacts business within the state;
> (3) owns property within the state; or
> (4) is personally served within the state.

QUESTION #1 (80%)

You are the law clerk for the judge to whose docket this case has been assigned. Draft a memorandum to the judge discussing all possibly relevant bases for dismissing any or all of the claims and parties in this lawsuit. Include in your memorandum all of the arguments that could be made in support of and in opposition to these bases for dismissal as well as your recommendation as to how each should be resolved.

QUESTION #2 (20%)

Now assume that Emillion had filed his lawsuit in state court in Lafayette. Also assume that Emillion brought all the same claims mentioned above against CBI, EIC, and Boudreaux. Before any other claims were filed, however, the three defendants had a meeting in which they agreed that they all would like to have the entire case adjudicated by a judge in the federal district court for the District of Delaware. Explain how and whether this could be accomplished.

CIVIL PROCEDURE
ESSAY EXAMINATION
ANSWERS

CIVIL PROCEDURE ESSAY EXAM #1

QUESTION #1

I. Hermione v. BDI

1. Choice of law — jurisdictional statute   Since suit was filed in federal court in Nevada, under Fed. R. Civ. P. 4(k)(1), in the absence of any federal jurisdictional provision, we look to the state jurisdictional statute for determining the statutory scope of personal jurisdiction.

2. Statutory basis for personal jurisdiction   The Nevada long-arm statute provides four possible bases for exercising personal jurisdiction. Since there is no indication that BDI was served in the forum state, or that it owns property located in Nevada, the only possibilities are provisions 1 and 2 of the statute.

Did BDI "commit a tortious act" in Nevada? If that statute is construed to require that the defendant's negligent act occurred in Nevada, then the answer is no because if BDI was negligent, its negligence occurred in the creation of the drug and/ or its failure to do appropriate testing, each of which happened in its lab in San Jose, California. On the other hand, if the statute is construed only to require that the defendant suffered the injury caused by the tortious act in the forum state, then the requirement is met since the plaintiff's husband ingested the pill in Nevada, became sick in Nevada, was hospitalized in Nevada, and died there.

Did BDI transact business within Nevada? BDI developed the drug in California and shipped those drugs to its distributor, APE, in Illinois. If the acts of its agent, APE, are imputed to BDI, then since APE distributes the drug nationwide, including in Nevada, BDI would be deemed to transact business within Nevada. Since at least one, and perhaps two, provisions of the jurisdictional statute are met, we must now determine whether application of the jurisdictional statute in this case comports with the constitutional requirements of the Due Process Clause of the Fourteenth Amendment.

3. Constitutionality of personal jurisdiction   Assuming, then, that the statute can apply to BDI, is the exercise of jurisdiction over BDI constitutional under the Due Process Clause of the Fourteenth Amendment? Supreme Court cases beginning with *International Shoe* instruct us to determine whether (a) the court is seeking to exercise general or specific jurisdiction; and (b) whether the defendant has created a purposeful relationship with the forum state and, if so, the nature and scope of that relationship.

Since the plaintiff is seeking to recover damages from taking the BDI drug, and since we have concluded that BDI was doing business in the forum state, the plaintiff's cause of action arises out of the defendant's relationship with the forum state and therefore the court is seeking to exercise specific jurisdiction.

Did BDI create a purposeful relationship with the forum state? Since this is a case, like *Volkswagen*, where the defendant did not deal directly with the plaintiff, and the defendant's product that allegedly damaged the plaintiff reached the forum through a chain of commerce, then we need to apply the stream of commerce standard to determine whether or not BDI purposefully availed itself of the benefits and protections of forum law, i.e., purposefully created a relationship with Nevada. Under the view of the stream of commerce test articulated by Justice O'Connor in *Asahi*, the plaintiff must establish that BDI not only placed its drug in the stream of commerce but took some affirmative step to direct it to the forum state of Nevada. In this case there is no evidence of any advertising or other direct conduct by BDI to market its product in Nevada. On the other hand, it purposefully entered into a distribution relationship with APE in which it knew, and relied upon the fact, that APE, the nation's second largest pharmaceutical distributor, would be distributing BDI's product in all 50 states, including Nevada. Consequently, it is likely to be concluded that BDI did purposefully create a relationship with the forum state.

What is the nature and scope of that relationship? Since APE, an agent of BDI, distributes the drug across the country, the facts suggest that this is a systematic and continuous relationship.

In light of the fact that the court is seeking to exercise specific jurisdiction, the extent of the relationship between the defendant and the forum state needs to meet a lower threshold than if the court was seeking to exercise general jurisdiction. In light of the apparently continuous nature of that relationship, the *International Shoe* portion of the constitutional requirements of personal jurisdiction would be satisfied.

Does the exercise of jurisdiction comport with the "fairness factors" articulated in *Volkswagen*? Having found that the *International Shoe* test of sufficient contacts has been satisfied, the Court in *Volkswagen* instructs us also to evaluate a quartet of other factors going to the reasonableness of exercising personal jurisdiction.

The interests of the plaintiff — the plaintiff has now returned to Florida and so presumably she has little interest, other than forum shopping, in a Nevada forum. Her interest in forum shopping for the most advantageous law is not a relevant factor here.

The interests of the forum — since the injured party was not a Nevada citizen and neither is the defendant, the state would have little interest in adjudicating this case other than the fact that the injury occurred there.

The interests of the judicial system — there is some interest in having the case tried in Nevada since those witnesses with information about the decedent's injury — the doctors and others in the hospital — are located in Nevada. But the witnesses relevant to the defendant's negligence are located in California.

The fairness factors certainly do not overwhelmingly support Nevada, but in light of the fact that this is a case of specific jurisdiction with significant defense contacts, the *Volkswagen* factors are not so overwhelming as to compel a conclusion of no jurisdiction.

4. Subject matter jurisdiction — federal question   FDA claim — this is a federal statutory claim and so jurisdiction lies under 28 U.S.C. §1331.

5. Subject matter jurisdiction — diversity of citizenship   Wrongful death claim — this is a state law claim. Can the court exercise diversity jurisdiction under 28 U.S.C. §1332(a)? The plaintiff is a citizen of Florida since that is the state of her permanent domicile. Under the definition of corporate citizenship for diversity purposes in 28 U.S.C. §1332(c), the defendant BDI is a citizen of Delaware, its state of incorporation, and California, the state of its principal place of business (ppb). Consequently, these two parties are diverse and the amount in controversy requirement of §1332(a) is met since the plaintiff's tort claim seeks damages in the amount of $15 million, which exceeds the statutory requirement of being in excess of $75,000. However, the plaintiff also has asserted a claim against defendant Stop & Shop which, like the plaintiff, is a citizen of Florida. Thus, there is no diversity between those two adverse parties. Pursuant to the Supreme Court's interpretation and application of the complete diversity doctrine in *Exxon Mobil*, where the plaintiff and one defendant are not diverse, this contaminates the entire suit and precludes diversity-based original jurisdiction over the entire civil action, even as to state law claims against defendants who are individually diverse from the plaintiff. Consequently, §1332 cannot serve as the basis for subject matter jurisdiction over this claim.

That requires us to assess whether or not the court can exercise supplemental jurisdiction over this state law claim because of the presence of a federal question claim by the plaintiff against this defendant. The question under §1367(a) is whether the two claims form part of the same Article III "case," i.e., whether they arise out of a common nucleus of operative fact. The federal question claim involves a determination of whether the defendant conducted sufficient study of the drug before marketing it. The state law claim is a wrongful death action alleging that the defendant acted negligently in its manufacture, inspection, distribution, and sale of the drug. These allegations involve some of the same events as the federal question and so the court probably will find that these two claims operate as part of a single Article III "case." Thus, subject to the discretionary factors set forth in §1367(c), the court will exercise supplemental jurisdiction over this claim. The state claim does not appear to raise novel or complex issues of state law or predominate over the federal claim as to justify the exercise of §1367(c) discretion to dismiss the state law claim.

6. Venue   In a multi-claim case, we look to the entirety of the suit to determine whether jurisdiction over the entire suit is based exclusively on diversity, i.e., whether each claim by a plaintiff should be examined under §1391(a) or (b). Since this case involves a federal question claim, jurisdiction is not based solely on diversity, and so venue must be examined for each claim brought by the plaintiffs under §1391(b). With respect to the federal question claim, venue lies in the district where the defendant resides or where a substantial part of the events occurred. Under §1391(c), a corporation "resides" for venue purposes in a district in which it is subject to personal jurisdiction. Since we determined already that BDI is subject to personal jurisdiction in Nevada, a one-district state, this requirement is met. Additionally, the ingestion of the drug, injury, and hospitalization all occurred in Las Vegas, which would meet the substantial part of events test as well. As to the diverse state law claim, again we look to §1391(b) and the answer here would be the same as for the federal question claim, for the same reason. So venue is proper for both claims.

7. Joinder of claims   There is no limit to the number of claims a plaintiff can join against a single defendant under Rule 18. So both claims are joinable.

II. Hermione v. APE

1. Statutory basis for personal jurisdiction The long-arm statute applies because APE is clearly transacting business in Nevada as it distributes nationwide. For the same reason mentioned with respect to BDI, APE could also be deemed to have committed a tortious act in Nevada based on the occurrence of the injury to the plaintiff's decedent there. Thus, there is a statutory basis for exercising personal jurisdiction over APE.

2. Constitutionality of personal jurisdiction APE clearly has a purposeful relationship with Nevada based on its distribution of goods there. The relationship is systematic and continuous. Because the plaintiff's cause of action arises out of APE's distribution of products in the forum, this is a case of specific jurisdiction. Since the relationship is systematic and continuous, the *International Shoe* test of sufficient contacts is met in this case of specific jurisdiction.

The fairness factors set forth in *Volkswagen* would play out the same here as with respect to BDI.

The interests of the plaintiff—the plaintiff has now returned to Florida and so presumably she has little interest, other than forum shopping, in a Nevada forum. Her interest in forum shopping for the most advantageous law is not a relevant factor here.

The interests of the forum — since the injured party was not a Nevada citizen and neither is the defendant, the state would have little interest in adjudicating this case other than the fact that the injury occurred there.

The interests of the judicial system — there is some interest in having the case tried in Nevada since those witnesses with information about the decedent's injury — the doctors and others in the hospital — are located in Nevada. But the witnesses relevant to the defendant's negligence are located in California.

The fairness factors certainly do not overwhelmingly support Nevada, but in light of the fact that this is a case of specific jurisdiction with significant defense contacts, the *Volkswagen* factors are not so overwhelming as to compel a conclusion of no jurisdiction.

3. Definition of corporate citizenship The defendant is a citizen, under §1332(c), of its state of incorporation, New York, and its state of principal place of business, which is Illinois since that is where its main warehouse is located.

4. Subject matter jurisdiction — diversity of citizenship The plaintiff has filed only one claim against APE — a state tort claim. The plaintiff is a citizen of Florida based on her permanent domicile there. The defendant is a citizen of New York and Illinois. Consequently, the two parties are diverse. The $15 million claim satisfies the jurisdictional amount in controversy requirement. However, the plaintiff also has asserted a claim against defendant Stop & Shop which, like the plaintiff, is a citizen of Florida. Thus, there is no diversity between those two adverse parties. Pursuant to the Supreme Court's interpretation and application of the complete diversity doctrine in *Exxon Mobil*, where the plaintiff and one defendant are not diverse, this contaminates the entire suit and precludes diversity-based original jurisdiction over the entire civil action, even as to state law claims against defendants who are individually diverse from the plaintiff. Consequently, §1332 cannot serve as the basis for subject matter jurisdiction over this state law claim.

That requires us to assess whether or not the court can exercise supplemental jurisdiction over this state law claim because of the presence of a federal question claim by the plaintiff against this defendant. The question under §1367(a) is whether the two claims form part of the same Article III "case," i.e., whether they arise out of a common nucleus of operative fact. The federal question claim against BDI involves a determination of whether the defendant conducted sufficient study of the drug before marketing it. The state law claim against APE, on the other hand, is a wrongful death action alleging that APE acted negligently in its distribution and sale of the drug. These allegations, therefore, arise out of different events than those involved in the federal question claim against BDI. Consequently, the court should find that these two claims do not operate as part of a single Article III "case." Thus, the court will not exercise supplemental jurisdiction over this claim. On the other hand, if the court takes a broad view of the facts giving rise to these two claims, then the remaining issue would be whether the court should decline to exercise supplemental jurisdiction pursuant to the discretionary factors set forth in §1367(c). As stated before, these factors do not support dismissal of the state law claim.

5. Venue   Most courts have concluded that the venue requirements do not have to be met with respect to claims that fall within the court's supplemental, as opposed to original, subject matter jurisdiction. So in most jurisdictions, a venue objection would not lie as to this claim. But where the courts do not adhere to this doctrine, the venue issue here would be governed by 18 U.S.C. §1391(b) since jurisdiction over this entire civil action is not based solely on diversity. Since the defendant is subject to personal jurisdiction in the forum state, a one-district state, it resides there for §1391 purposes and so meets that requirement. Additionally, the ingestion of the drug, injury, and hospitalization all occurred in Las Vegas, which would meet the substantial part of events test as well. Venue lies over this claim in Nevada.

6. Joinder of parties   Rule 20 permits a plaintiff to join multiple parties if (1) the defendant asserts against them a right to relief arising out of a common series of transactions or occurrences; and (2) there is a single question of law or fact common to the plaintiff's claims against the joined defendants.

The plaintiff's claims arise out of the creation and distribution of a drug and this set of transactions is common to her claims against both BDI and APE. Additionally, the issue of the extent of the plaintiff's injury is common to both claims. Thus, both requirements of Rule 20 are satisfied and APE can be properly joined as a defendant.

III. Hermione v. Stop & Shop

1. Statutory basis of personal jurisdiction   This drugstore in Miami is a nonresident of the forum. It does not transact any business in Nevada. The tortious act provision of the long-arm statute will be deemed to apply if the tortious act is construed to mean the occurrence of the injury. It will not apply if the statute is interpreted to require the defendant's negligent act to have occurred in the forum. If neither statutory provision applies, then there will be no basis for exercising personal jurisdiction over Stop & Shop. But if the tortious act provision applies, then we must turn to the constitutional inquiry.

2. Constitutionality of personal jurisdiction   With respect to the constitutional inquiry under *International Shoe*, Stop & Shop does not appear to have created a purposeful relationship with the forum state. Like the retailer in *Volkswagen*, it did nothing to place the product in the stream of commerce or push it toward Nevada. It sold the product in Florida and the plaintiff unilaterally took the product and used it in Nevada, like the VW car in *Volkswagen*. Consequently, under the O'Connor analysis in *Asahi*, Stop & Shop would not meet the stream of commerce test and would be found not to have created a purposeful relationship with the forum state. Under the Brennan view in *Asahi*, the fact that the good it sold was taken, used, and produced an injury in the forum state would be sufficient. So even if this is viewed as an attempt to exercise specific jurisdiction, the absence of affiliating circumstances under the O'Connor stream of commerce test would be dispositive. No jurisdiction because of the absence of a purposeful relationship.

Assuming, nevertheless, we adopted the Brennan view and needed, therefore, to evaluate the *Volkswagen* fairness factors, i.e., we concluded that Stop & Shop had created a purposeful relationship with Nevada, the closeness of this case would suggest that the fairness factors would push us toward a conclusion of no jurisdiction.

The interests of the plaintiff — the plaintiff has now returned to Florida and so presumably she has little interest, other than forum shopping, in a Nevada forum. Her interest in forum shopping for the most advantageous law is not a relevant factor here.

The interests of the forum — since the injured party was not a Nevada citizen and neither is the defendant, the state would have little interest in adjudicating this case other than the fact that the injury occurred there.

The interests of the judicial system — there is some interest in having the case tried in Nevada since those witnesses with information about the decedent's injury — the doctors and others in the hospital — are located in Nevada. But the witnesses relevant to the defendant's negligence are located in California.

3. Subject matter jurisdiction   Both the plaintiff and the defendant are citizens of Florida. Consequently, there is no diversity jurisdiction over the single state law tort claim brought by the plaintiff against Stop & Shop. And the fact that these two parties are nondiverse means, per the Supreme Court's ruling in *Exxon Mobil*, that diversity over the entire suit has been contaminated and §1332 cannot provide a basis for original jurisdiction over any claim in this suit.

But does this state law tort claim fall within the court's supplemental jurisdiction under §1367? The plaintiff does have a §1331 (FDA) claim against defendant BDI. But to meet the requirement of §1367(a), this tort claim and the FDA claim against BDI would have to arise out of a common nucleus of operative fact, i.e., constitute part of the same "case or controversy." The FDA claim against BDI arises out of a failure to inspect. The tort claim against Stop & Shop is presumably based on its failure to inspect the contents of the product it sold. These two claims do not arise out of a common nucleus of operative fact. Therefore, there should be no §1367(a) supplemental jurisdiction.

Since the lack of diversity between Stop & Shop and the plaintiff destroyed the possibility of complete diversity in this civil action, there is no claim in this suit that would fall under the court's original §1332 jurisdiction. Consequently, there can be no assessment of whether or not supplemental jurisdiction over this tort claim could be exercised under §1367(b).

4. Venue   Venue would not lie under §1391(b). Stop & Shop does not reside in Nevada and a substantial part of the events relating to this claim did not arise in Nevada. So no venue under §1391(b)(1) or (2). Subsection 3 would not apply since venue would lie in Miami.

5. Joinder of parties   Is this defendant joinable? Under Rule 20, there is a common question of fact present in this claim — the extent of the plaintiff's injury. If this defendant's retail sale is viewed as part of a series of transactions common to the claims against the other two defendants, then joinder would be permitted. But it would not matter since there is no personal jurisdiction over this defendant and no subject matter jurisdiction over the claim.

IV. BDI v. Johnson

1. Statutory basis of personal jurisdiction   Johnson, a California citizen, does not transact business or own property within Nevada. He could only meet the tortious act requirement for statutory jurisdiction if that statute is construed to require only that the injury resulting from the tortious act occurs within the forum.

2. Constitutionality of personal jurisdiction   Johnson is so tangentially connected to the stream of commerce that he would certainly not fall within the O'Connor-defined stream of commerce test in *Asahi* and probably also would not meet the Brennan totality of circumstances requirement.

Plus, this would be an attempt at general jurisdiction since BDI's indemnity claim does not arise out of any connection that Johnson would have with Nevada through the stream of commerce since it arises out of his scientific activity in California.

3. Subject matter jurisdiction — diversity of citizenship   Both of these third-party claims, the indemnity and reimbursement claims, are state law–based tort claims. The parties are nondiverse since Johnson is a citizen of California, his state of permanent domicile, and BDI is a corporate citizen of California, the state of its principal place of business. So no §1332 jurisdiction.

4. Subject matter jurisdiction — supplemental jurisdiction   Since both of these third-party claims are nondiverse state law claims, can the court exercise supplemental jurisdiction over either or both of them as supplemental to the one federal question (original jurisdiction) claim in the case? BDI's indemnity claim against Johnson, by definition, arises out of the facts that gave rise to the plaintiff's FDA (federal question) claim against BDI. Thus, supplemental jurisdiction will exist under §1367(a). The question then becomes whether the discretionary considerations in §1367(c) argue against exercising supplemental jurisdiction. The indemnity claim does not appear to raise a novel state law issue or create undue jury confusion or predominate over the plaintiff's diversity claim.

The claim to recover reimbursement for fraudulent expenses, a nondiverse state law claim, would not qualify for supplemental jurisdiction since it does not arise out of a common nucleus of operative fact that gave rise to the plaintiff's FDA claim against BDI.

5. Venue   Venue would not lie over this claim. Johnson does not reside in Nevada and the events giving rise to this claim did not occur in Nevada. The catch-all answer of §1391(b)(3) is unavailable since venue would lie over this claim in another district — a district in California.

6. Joinder of claims   Under Rule 14(a), the indemnity claim would be a joinable third-party claim but the claim for reimbursement would not be joinable since it does not seek indemnity or contribution.

7. Joinder of parties   The third-party defendant can be joined since the indemnity claim meets the requirements of Rule 20.

QUESTION #2

I. Hermione v. BDI and Stop & Shop

1. Removal   There is federal subject matter jurisdiction over both claims against BDI. The FDA claim falls within the court's original jurisdiction under §1331 while the state claim falls within its supplemental jurisdiction under §1367(a). The courts have concluded that this entire part of the case can be removed. The analysis is that the federal question claim is removable under §1441(a) because it falls within the court's subject matter jurisdiction and that the federal court can then exercise supplemental jurisdiction over the nondiverse (because of lack of complete diversity between the plaintiff and the two defendants) state law claim. And the state law wrongful death claim arises out of the same alleged failure to adequately test the product as the federal question claim. Thus, neither claim will be remanded.

The plaintiff's claim against Stop & Shop is a nondiverse state law claim. This raises the question of whether §1441(a)'s statement limiting removal to cases within the court's original jurisdiction includes claims within the court's supplemental jurisdiction. The cases indicate that the answer to this is yes.

Does the state law claim against Stop & Shop fall within the court's supplemental jurisdiction? To meet the requirement of §1367(a), this tort claim against Stop & Shop and the plaintiff's §1331 FDA claim against BDI would have to arise out of a common nucleus of operative fact, i.e., constitute part of the same "case or controversy." The FDA claim arises out of a failure to inspect. The tort claim against Stop & Shop is presumably based on its failure to inspect the contents of the product it sold. These two claims do not arise out of a common nucleus of operative fact. Therefore, there can be no §1367(a) supplemental jurisdiction.

Is there supplemental jurisdiction under §1367(b)? The short answer is no because pursuant to the ruling in *Exxon Mobil*, the presence of the nondiverse defendant Stop & Shop contaminated the diversity between the plaintiff and BDI and so there is no original jurisdiction over any state law claim in this suit under §1332. Thus, if there is no original jurisdiction under §1332, there can be no investigation of supplemental jurisdiction under §1367(b).

So the claim against Stop & Shop is not removable under §1441(a). Is it removable under §1441(c)? Section 1441(c) authorizes removal of a nonremovable claim when it is separate and independent from a federal question (§1331) claim.

The negligence claim against Stop & Shop is separate and independent from the plaintiff's FDA claim against BDI since disposition of the FDA claim will not determine the disposition of the tort claim. Thus, the tort claim against Stop & Shop falls within the provisions of §1441(c) and can be removed. But §1441(c) also gives the federal judge discretion to remand the state law claim against Stop & Shop and keep the clearly removable claims against BDI.

QUESTION #3

I. Justine Long v. BDI

1. Issue preclusion   The plaintiff in this suit is seeking to preclude the defendant from relitigating the issues raised in its defenses, the same defenses that were unsuccessfully raised by that same defendant in the prior suit brought by a different plaintiff.

The plaintiff, therefore, is seeking to invoke the doctrine of issue preclusion. This is not a case involving claim preclusion since the parties to the two lawsuits are different.

Since the plaintiff was not a party to the first lawsuit, this is a case of non-mutual issue preclusion or non-mutual collateral estoppel. And since it is the plaintiff seeking to invoke the doctrine by seeking to preclude the defendant from relitigating the issues of its negligence, this is an attempt to invoke offensive non-mutual collateral estoppel.

Offensive non-mutual collateral estoppel is generally not permitted when the court concludes either (1) that the plaintiff could easily have joined in the first lawsuit (so as not to encourage "wait and see" plaintiffs) or (2) that invoking issue preclusion would be unfair to the party against whom it is being invoked such as where the defendant did not have incentive to try its best in the first lawsuit. Lack of incentive could occur where the stakes were much lower in the first lawsuit brought against the defendant or where the second suit provides the defendant procedural opportunities that were not available in the first action that could cause a different result.

Since this plaintiff's claims arise out of the same transactions or occurrences that gave rise to Hermione's suit, i.e., the defendant's negligent manufacture of the drug, the first requirement of Rule 20 is met. Second, the issue of BDI's negligence is common to both lawsuits. Consequently, both requirements of Rule 20 are met, which means that Justine could have joined in Hermione's lawsuit. Therefore, the court will not permit the invocation of offensive non-mutual collateral estoppel.

The presence of other potential plaintiffs was not unforeseeable to the defendant. The stakes in Hermione's suit were high. There is no evidence of lack of procedural opportunities in the first case. Therefore, there is no evidence of unfairness to the defendant. Nevertheless, since the plaintiff could have joined in the first suit, under the rule articulated in *Parklane Hosiery*, the court will not invoke offensive non-mutual collateral estoppel.

CIVIL PROCEDURE ESSAY EXAM #2

QUESTION #1

I. Plaintiffs Pat and Leslie v. HFI

1. Choice of law—jurisdictional statute   Per Fed. R. Civ. P. 4(k)(1), in the absence of an applicable federal jurisdiction statute, we look to the forum law's long-arm statute to determine the statutory sufficiency of personal jurisdiction.

2. Statutory basis of personal jurisdiction   Does the New Mexico long-arm statute provide for personal jurisdiction over HFI? Since there is no evidence that the defendant was personally served or owns property in New Mexico, the issues are whether or not it either transacts business or committed a tortious act within New Mexico. HFI has shareowners in every state, therefore in New Mexico. To the extent that it communicates and does business with them, it satisfies this portion of the statute.

Whether or not it also meets the "tortious act" provision depends upon the construction of that statute. If it is interpreted to require the negligent act to have occurred within the forum state, the statute will not apply since HFI's conduct occurred in California. But if the statute is construed to require only that the resultant injury occur in the forum, then it would apply since readers of the prospectus in New Mexico were injured when they read it there. In either event, at least one provision of the statute will apply to HFI, which mandates consideration of the constitutionality of exercising personal jurisdiction over this entity in New Mexico.

3. Constitutionality of personal jurisdiction   Having found that the statute applies, the next question is whether the application of that statute in this case is consistent with the due process requirements of the Fourteenth Amendment. The first portion of this test is the *International Shoe* contacts inquiry. This is a twofold inquiry. First, to what extent, if at all, did the defendant create and maintain a purposeful relationship with the forum state? Second, is the court seeking to exert general or specific jurisdiction?

The facts indicate that it has shareholders in the forum, which means that it is directly involved with them in the forum state. It also is listed in NASDAQ, which means that its stock is offered for sale by stock brokerages in New Mexico. The facts also state that it markets and services its products nationwide. All of these facts suggest a purposeful relationship and a systematic and continuous relationship.

The court is exerting specific jurisdiction since the plaintiff's claims arise out of these activities by HFI in the forum state.

The second portion of the constitutional test is the application of the "fairness factors" outlined in *Volkswagen*.

One of the two plaintiffs is a forum citizen, which suggests that at least this plaintiff has an interest in having the case litigated in New Mexico. The forum state also has an interest in providing a forum for those of its citizens victimized by HFI's activities. The overall judicial system has less of an efficiency interest in having the case heard in New Mexico since the center of gravity of the case, in terms of the location of most witnesses, is not in New Mexico. But this is not sufficient to overwhelm the result of the *International Shoe* contacts inquiry. Therefore, the courts of New Mexico can constitutionally exercise personal jurisdiction over HFI.

4. Subject matter jurisdiction — federal question   One of the two claims is a federal question declaratory judgment claim and so there is jurisdiction over it under §1331.

5. Subject matter jurisdiction — diversity of citizenship   The non-declaratory judgment claim is a $50,000 state law tort claim. Plaintiff Pat is a citizen of Pennsylvania and Plaintiff Leslie is a citizen of New Mexico on the basis of their permanent domicile in these two states. HFI is a citizen of Delaware and California under the definition of corporate citizenship in §1332(c). So all of these adverse parties are of diverse citizenship. However, defendant accounting firm DCH is, like one of the plaintiffs, a citizen of Pennsylvania. Accordingly, the presence of this nondiverse defendant, pursuant to the Court's ruling in *Exxon Mobil*, contaminates the existence of diversity jurisdiction by destroying complete diversity. This, in turn, means that diversity cannot serve as the basis for original jurisdiction over any of the plaintiffs' claims. Consequently, even though the plaintiffs are diverse from HFI, the lack of complete diversity means that §1332 cannot serve as the basis for original jurisdiction over the state law claim brought against HFI by the plaintiffs. But what about supplemental jurisdiction?

6. Subject matter jurisdiction — supplemental jurisdiction   Since the court cannot exercise diversity jurisdiction over the state law claim asserted against HFI, we must examine whether the court can exercise supplemental jurisdiction over the plaintiffs' state law tort claims against HFI under §1367(a). The question under §1367(a) is whether the plaintiffs' federal question and tort claims against HFI form part of the same Article III "case," i.e., whether they arise out of a common nucleus of operative fact. The federal question claim alleges the filing of false and misleading statements with the SEC while the tort claim alleges fraud in connection with that same activity. Consequently, the two claims do form part of the same case and, therefore, subject to the discretionary considerations set forth in §1367(c), the court will exercise supplemental jurisdiction over the state law claim. None of the factors set forth in §1367(c) that would justify dismissal of the state law claim is present here since there is no suggestion that the state law claim predominates or is a question of first impression. So the court should exercise supplemental jurisdiction over this claim.

7. Venue   Since the plaintiffs assert a federal question claim in this civil action, subject matter jurisdiction over it is not based solely on diversity of citizenship. Thus, each claim in the case must have venue determined under the terms of §1391(b). With respect to the plaintiff's §1331 claim, under §1391(b), venue would lie in the chosen forum of New Mexico because the defendant HFI "resides" there within the meaning of §1391(c) since it is subject to personal jurisdiction in this one-district state. With respect to the state law claim, most courts have ruled that claims falling within a court's supplemental jurisdiction do not have to meet the statutory venue requirements. For those who do hold supplemental claims subject to venue requirements, under §1391(b), venue over the supplemental claim would lie in New Mexico because the defendant HFI "resides" there within the meaning of §1391(c) since it is subject to personal jurisdiction in this one-district state.

8. Joinder of parties   Joinder of the two plaintiffs is permitted under Rule 20 because they assert claims that arise out of a common series of events and there is a common question of law or fact asserted by each of them against the defendant HFI — the false and misleading nature of the earnings report.

II. Plaintiffs Pat and Leslie v. Defendant DCH

1. Statutory basis of personal jurisdiction   Under Rule 4(k)(1), we look to New Mexico's jurisdictional provision. Whether or not it meets the "tortious act" provision depends upon the construction of that statute. If it is interpreted to require the negligent act to have occurred within the forum state, the statute will not apply since DCH's conduct occurred in California. But if the statute is construed to require only that the resultant injury occur in the forum, then it would apply since readers of the prospectus in New Mexico were injured when they read it there.

The facts do not indicate whether or not DCH also has clients or otherwise does business in New Mexico. So the best bet for statutory jurisdiction is the "tortious act" provision.

2. Constitutionality of personal jurisdiction   Assuming the existence of statutory jurisdiction, the next question is whether the application of that statute in this case is consistent with the due process requirements of the Fourteenth Amendment. The first portion of this test is the *International Shoe* contacts inquiry. This is a twofold inquiry. First, to what extent, if at all, did the defendant create and maintain a purposeful relationship with the forum state? Second, is the court seeking to exert general or specific jurisdiction?

While DCH does not have any direct contacts with New Mexico, it could be viewed as part of the chain of commerce with respect to HFI's distribution of earnings reports. It prepared a report that it knew would be publicly circulated to HFI's shareholders, some of whom live in the forum state. Is this enough? Under the O'Connor stream of commerce standard set forth in *Asahi*, it would not be enough since the defendant, to create a purposeful relationship with the forum state, would have to have done something specifically to target the New Mexico market. It does not appear to have done so. Under the Brennan alternative model of the stream of commerce test, the fact that the injury was suffered by the consumer of this information in the forum would be enough.

Assuming we concluded that there was a purposeful relationship, and we acknowledge that this is an example of specific jurisdiction, since the claim arises out of the presence of these misleading reports in the forum, the limited nature of DCH's contacts with the forum, i.e., its connection to the chain of commerce that resulted in the distribution of the reports in the forum state, might be enough to satisfy the constitutional requirement of "minimum" contacts.

Assuming we find that the two-part *International Shoe* test has been satisfied, we move to the "fairness" factors set forth in *Volkswagen*. One of the two plaintiffs is a forum citizen, which suggests that at least this plaintiff has an interest in having the case litigated in New Mexico. The forum state also has an interest in providing a forum for those of its citizens victimized by HFI's activities. The overall judicial system has less of an efficiency interest in having the case heard in New Mexico since the center of gravity of the case, in terms of the location of most witnesses, is not in New Mexico. Since the *International Shoe* test was only marginally supportive of jurisdiction, these factors push a bit stronger in favor of exercising jurisdiction.

3. Subject matter jurisdiction — diversity of citizenship   The plaintiffs assert only a state law claim against DCH. DCH is a citizen of Pennsylvania and California based on its state of incorporation and principal place of business, respectively. Since Plaintiff Pat is also a citizen of Pennsylvania, there is no diversity between these two adverse parties. Consequently, no §1332 diversity-based jurisdiction exists over Pat's state law claim against DCH.

Leslie is diverse from DCH since she is a citizen of New Mexico. But her $50,000 state law claim does not meet the jurisdictional amount in controversy requirement, so the fact that Plaintiff Leslie is diverse from DCH is of no avail. The two plaintiffs cannot aggregate the value of their tort law claims against DCH because separate plaintiffs cannot aggregate the value of their claims against a common defendant to meet the amount in controversy requirement. Thus, since there is no §1332 basis for jurisdiction over this claim, we turn to the possibility of exercising supplemental jurisdiction.

4. Subject matter jurisdiction — supplemental jurisdiction   Since there is no diversity jurisdiction over either plaintiff's state claims, what about supplemental jurisdiction under §1367? Under §1367(a), supplemental jurisdiction would be available if the plaintiffs' state law claims against DCH were deemed to be part of the same case as their federal claim against HFI, i.e., derived from a common nucleus of operative fact. This would be an attempt at what used to be called pendent party jurisdiction. It is permitted under §1367(a) since there is a federal question claim and the nondiverse state law claims and the federal claim arise out of a common nucleus of operative events — the alleged misrepresentations in the annual reports that were made publicly available. Under §1367(c), the federal court would have the discretion not to exercise supplemental jurisdiction over the state claims if they raised novel issues of state law, predominated over the federal question, or created the potential for jury confusion. None of these factors appear present in this case. Therefore, the court would exercise supplemental jurisdiction over these nondiverse state law claims.

5. Venue   Most courts have ruled that claims falling within a court's supplemental jurisdiction do not have to meet the statutory venue requirements. For those who do hold supplemental claims subject to venue requirements, under §1391(a), venue over this state law claim would lie in New Mexico because the defendant DCH "resides" there within the meaning of §1391(c) if, as we have determined, it is subject to personal jurisdiction in this one-district state.

6. Joinder of parties defendant   Under Rule 20, plaintiffs can join multiple defendants if the claims asserted against those defendants arise out of a common transaction or occurrence and if one question of law or fact is common to the claims against each defendant. Both of these requirements are met since the claims by the plaintiffs against both HFI and DCH arise out of the misrepresentations in the earnings report and there is a common question of fact—i.e., did the statements contain misrepresentations?

III. Pat and Leslie v. Snerdley

1. Statutory basis for personal jurisdiction Snerdley, a citizen of California, based on his permanent domicile there (his other homes are only vacation homes), has no direct contact with New Mexico. He, unlike his corporation, is not doing business there. Whether or not he meets the "tortious act" provision depends upon the construction of that statute. If it is interpreted to require the negligent act to have occurred within the forum state, the statute will not apply since his conduct occurred in California. But if the statute is construed to require only that the resultant injury occur in the forum, then it would apply since readers of the prospectus that he authorized were injured in New Mexico when they read it there. If the statute covers him, then we must examine the constitutionality of exercising personal jurisdiction over him in New Mexico.

2. Constitutionality of personal jurisdiction Assuming the existence of statutory jurisdiction, the next question is whether the application of that statute in this case is consistent with the due process requirements of the Fourteenth Amendment. The first portion of this test is the *International Shoe* contacts inquiry. This is a twofold inquiry. First, to what extent, if at all, did the defendant create and maintain a purposeful relationship with the forum state? Second, is the court seeking to exert general or specific jurisdiction?

Snerdley does not have any direct contacts with New Mexico. But he could be viewed as a part of the chain of commerce with respect to HFI's distribution of earnings reports. He authorized the preparation and distribution of a report that he knew would be publicly circulated to HFI's shareholders, some of whom live in the forum state. Is this enough? Under the O'Connor stream of commerce standard set forth in *Asahi*, it would not be enough since the defendant, to create a purposeful relationship with the forum state, would have to have done something specifically to target the New Mexico market. It does not appear to have done so. Under the Brennan alternative model of the stream of commerce test, the fact that the injury was suffered by the consumer of this information in the forum would be enough.

Assuming we concluded that there was a purposeful relationship, and we acknowledge that this is an example of specific jurisdiction, since the claim arises out of the presence of these misleading reports in the forum, the limited nature of Snerdley's contacts with the forum, i.e., his connection to the chain of commerce that resulted in the distribution of the reports in the forum state, might be enough to satisfy the constitutional requirement of "minimum" contacts.

Assuming we find that the two-part *International Shoe* test has been satisfied, we move to the "fairness" factors set forth in *Volkswagen*. One of the two plaintiffs is a forum citizen, which suggests that at least this plaintiff has an interest in having the case litigated in New Mexico. The forum state also has an interest in providing a forum for those of its citizens victimized by HFI's activities. The overall judicial system has less of an efficiency interest in having the case heard in New Mexico since the center of gravity of the case, in terms of the location of most witnesses, is not in New Mexico. Since the *International Shoe* test was only marginally supportive of jurisdiction, these factors push a bit stronger in favor of exercising jurisdiction.

3. Subject matter jurisdiction — diversity of citizenship   With respect to the state law claim by both plaintiffs, there is complete diversity. Snerdley is a citizen of California. The plaintiffs are citizens of Pennsylvania and New Mexico. But the two plaintiffs' tort claims do not meet §1332(a)'s jurisdictional amount in controversy requirement of being in excess of $75,000. So neither of these two claims falls within the court's diversity jurisdiction. And the value of each of these two claims cannot be aggregated together because plaintiffs cannot aggregate the value of their claims against a common defendant to meet the amount in controversy requirement. Moreover, the presence of the nondiverse defendant DCH destroyed complete diversity and, under *Exxon Mobil*, removed the possibility of diversity as the basis for exercising original jurisdiction over any claims brought by the plaintiffs. Thus, we must turn to supplemental jurisdiction.

4. Subject matter jurisdiction — supplemental jurisdiction   Since there is no diversity jurisdiction over the state claims, what about supplemental jurisdiction over this state law fraud claim under §1367? Under §1367(a), supplemental jurisdiction would be available if the state and federal claims were part of the same case, i.e., derived from a common nucleus of operative fact. That requirement is met since they both arise out of the alleged misrepresentations in the annual reports that were made publicly available. Under §1367(c), the federal court would have the discretion not to exercise supplemental jurisdiction over the state claims if they raised novel issues of state law, predominated over the federal question, or created the potential for jury confusion. None of these factors appear present in this case. Therefore, the court would exercise supplemental jurisdiction over these nondiverse state law claims.

5. Venue   Most courts have ruled that claims falling within a court's supplemental jurisdiction do not have to meet the statutory venue requirements. For those who do hold supplemental claims subject to venue requirements, under §1391(a), venue over the federal claim would lie in New Mexico because the defendant Snerdley does not reside there since he resides in Malibu, California, and none of his other homes is in New Mexico. And whatever conduct he engaged in relative to this suit happened either where he lives or in one of the offices of HFI, none of which are in New Mexico. Hence, if the venue analysis needs to be undertaken, venue would not lie in New Mexico for this claim.

6. Joinder of parties defendant   Under Rule 20, plaintiffs can join multiple defendants if the claims asserted against those defendants arise out of a common transaction or occurrence and if one question of law or fact is common to the claims against each defendant. Both of these requirements are met since the claims by the plaintiffs against HFI, DCH, and Snerdley arise out of the misrepresentations in the earnings report and there is a common question of fact — i.e., did the statements contain misrepresentations?

IV. HFI v. DCH

1. Subject matter jurisdiction — diversity of citizenship   This is a cross-claim seeking indemnity under state law. HFI is a citizen of Delaware and California and DCH is a citizen of Pennsylvania and California. So there is no diversity between the adverse parties to this cross-claim. Thus, we must turn to supplemental jurisdiction.

2. Subject matter jurisdiction — supplemental jurisdiction   Since the indemnity claim is a nondiverse state law claim, can the court assert supplemental jurisdiction over it under §1367? The answer is yes since this indemnity claim, by definition, arises out of the same nucleus of fact that gave rise to the plaintiffs' federal claim against HFI.

There is a different answer for the breach of contract claim. It is also a nondiverse state claim but there is no supplemental jurisdiction because it is totally unrelated to the plaintiffs' claim against HFI.

3. Venue   The governing common law rule is that there is no independent necessity for venue over claims that fall within the court's supplemental jurisdiction. For those jurisdictions who do hold supplemental claims subject to venue requirements, under §1391(a), venue would lie in New Mexico because DCH "resides" there within the meaning of §1391(c) because it is subject to personal jurisdiction in this one-district state.

4. Joinder of claims   The indemnity claim is a joinable cross-claim under Rule 13(g) because it is transactionally related to the plaintiffs' claim against HFI as it is a claim for indemnity from damages recovered by the plaintiff. But the breach of contract claim is not joinable under Rule 13(g) because it is not transactionally related to the plaintiffs' claim against HFI.

V. DCH v. Goff

1. Statutory basis for personal jurisdiction   Goff is presumably a resident and citizen of California since that is where DCH's main offices are. She is not doing business in New Mexico and could only be subject to the tortious act provision of the long-arm statute if that statute is construed to apply when the injury, rather than the negligent act, occurred there.

2. Constitutionality of personal jurisdiction   Assuming she meets the statutory test for jurisdiction, Goff fails the constitutional standard. She has no direct contact with the forum state of New Mexico and DCH's relationships with New Mexico cannot be imputed to her. Therefore, in the absence of any relationship with the forum, there is no constitutional basis for exercising personal jurisdiction over her.

3. Subject matter jurisdiction — diversity of citizenship   This is a third-party complaint for indemnity, a claim arising under state law. Goff is a citizen of California and DCH is a citizen of California and Pennsylvania. So there is no federal claim and no diversity.

4. Subject matter jurisdiction — supplemental jurisdiction   Since the indemnity claim is a nondiverse state law claim, could the court exercise supplemental jurisdiction under §1367? This indemnity claim is part of the same cause of action that the plaintiffs have against DCH. Since there is supplemental jurisdiction over the plaintiffs' claims against DCH, it would extend to this claim by DCH for indemnity.

5. Venue   There is no independent requirement for venue over an indemnity claim.

6. Joinder of claims   This third-party complaint for indemnity is joinable under Rule 14(a).

VI. Snerdley v. Pat and Leslie

1. Statutory basis for personal jurisdiction   Plaintiffs have consented to the exercise of personal jurisdiction over them by filing the complaint.

2. Constitutionality of personal jurisdiction   No constitutional issue here since the plaintiffs have consented to the exercise of jurisdiction over them by filing the complaint.

3. Subject matter jurisdiction — diversity of citizenship   Snerdley is a citizen of California. Pat is a citizen of Pennsylvania and Leslie is a citizen of New Mexico. Therefore, there is complete diversity of citizenship. But the $65,000 claim does not meet the jurisdictional amount in controversy requirement. He cannot aggregate the value of the claims against each counter-defendant since a moving party cannot aggregate the value of claims against separate defendants. Thus, there is no diversity jurisdiction over this state claim under either §1331 or §1332.

4. Subject matter jurisdiction — supplemental jurisdiction   Since this state law claim does not meet the amount in controversy requirement for diversity jurisdiction, can the court exercise supplemental jurisdiction under §1367? This claim does not constitute part of the same case as the plaintiffs' claims against Snerdley since it does not arise out of the common nucleus of facts that gave rise to the plaintiffs' claims, since it does not arise out of the allegedly misrepresented earnings reports. The fact that his defamation claim arises out of their bringing this suit against him is not sufficient to establish supplemental jurisdiction.

5. Venue   Since there is no subject matter jurisdiction, there is no issue of venue.

6. Joinder of claims   There is no limit on joinability of counterclaims under Rule 13.

 QUESTION #2

I. Pat and Leslie v. HFI, DCH, and Snerdley

1. Removal   The plaintiffs' federal question claim against HFI is removable. The state claim against HFI is removable because it falls within the court's supplemental jurisdiction and supplemental claims are removable under §1441(a).

The nondiverse state law claims by the plaintiffs against DCH would also be removable under §1441(a) because they fall within the court's supplemental jurisdiction.

The plaintiffs' nondiverse state law claims against Snerdley would be removable under §1441(a) because they fall within the court's supplemental jurisdiction.

If, for any reason, the court determined that it did not have supplemental jurisdiction over any of these nondiverse state law claims, the removability of these otherwise nonremovable claims would be governed by §1441(c), which permits removability where the nonremovable claim is separate and independent from a §1331 claim. We have a §1331 claim here — the declaratory judgment claim. The problem is that the claims against the defendants are not separate and independent from the §1331 claim since the resolution of that claim would have a bearing on the resolution of the state claims.

QUESTION #3

I. SEC v. HFI and DCH

1. Claim preclusion   Since the defendants are seeking to have the plaintiff SEC's entire claim dismissed, they are seeking to invoke the doctrine of claim preclusion (res judicata). But the prime requirement for invoking res judicata/claim preclusion is that the parties to both suits are the same. It is unconstitutional under the Due Process Clause to preclude someone from bringing a claim based on a prior adjudication as to which they were not a party. That is precisely what the defendants are seeking to do here and, therefore, they will be unsuccessful.

CIVIL PROCEDURE ESSAY EXAM #3

QUESTION #1

I. Diamond v. Humanity

1. Choice of law — jurisdictional statute   Under Rule 4(k)(1), since there is no applicable federal jurisdictional statute, we look to the long-arm statute of the forum state to determine if there is a statutory basis for personal jurisdiction.

2. Statutory basis for personal jurisdiction   Although Humanity's operations seem to be centered around Ohio, they did negotiate an agreement with Diamond, a company whose headquarters are located in Indiana. The contract was conducted through an exchange of email and fax transmissions that were sent to and from Humanity's executive offices in Indiana. There were also three phone conversations that Humanity employees in Ohio had with Diamond supervisors in Indiana concerning how to perform their job and on one occasion, a Humanity employee had to meet with Diamond supervisors in Indiana to solve a problem. All of these facts indicate that Humanity met the statutory requirement of "transacting business within the state" as contained in the Indiana long-arm statute.

There is no evidence that any other provision of the long-arm statute applies to Humanity. But satisfying one provision is enough.

3. Constitutionality of personal jurisdiction   Having determined the existence of statutory jurisdiction, we now must determine whether the exercise of that jurisdiction is consistent with the due process requirements of the Fourteenth Amendment.

The first portion of this test is the *International Shoe* contacts inquiry. This is a twofold inquiry. First, to what extent, if at all, did the defendant create and maintain a purposeful relationship with the forum state? Second, is the court seeking to exert general or specific jurisdiction?

Although Humanity's operations seem to be centered around Ohio, they did negotiate an agreement with Diamond, a company whose headquarters are located in Indiana. The contract was conducted through an exchange of email and fax transmissions that were sent to and from Humanity's executive offices in Indiana. There were also three phone conversations that Humanity employees in Ohio had with Diamond supervisors in Indiana concerning how to perform their job and on one occasion a Humanity employee had to meet with Diamond supervisors in Indiana to solve a problem. All of these facts indicate that Humanity has purposefully availed itself of the benefits and protections of Indiana law and that these contacts are more than isolated.

With respect to the second portion of the *International Shoe* contacts assessment, the court is being asked to exercise specific jurisdiction since Diamond's claim against Humanity is for breach of the contract the negotiation of which created the contacts between Humanity and the forum state. Therefore, the plaintiff's claim arose out of the defendant's contacts with the forum state.

Since the court is being asked to assert specific jurisdiction, a lower threshold of contacts is sufficient to meet the *International Shoe* test. The affiliating relationship between Humanity and Indiana in the form of the contacts undertaken to negotiate and implement the contract meet the *Shoe* test for constitutionality for specific jurisdiction.

The second portion of the constitutional test is the application of the "fairness factors" outlined in *Volkswagen*. The plaintiff has an interest in an Indiana forum since it is a forum citizen. The forum state has an interest in providing a forum for the enforcement of contracts entered into by its citizens. The interstate judicial system has an efficiency interest in Indiana as the forum since much of the evidence, by way of testimony of Diamond's president and other executives, is found in Indiana. Therefore, the *Volkswagen* fairness factors further support the exercise of personal jurisdiction over Humanity.

4. Subject matter jurisdiction — definition of corporate citizenship   Diamond's claim against Humanity is a state law claim. Under the definition of corporate citizenship for diversity jurisdiction purposes found in 28 U.S.C. §1332(c), Humanity is a citizen of Ohio, its state of incorporation and its principal place of business. Ohio is its principal place of business because its corporate headquarters are located there.

5. Subject matter jurisdiction — diversity of citizenship   This is a state law claim. Under the definition of corporate citizenship for diversity jurisdiction purposes found in 28 U.S.C. §1332(c), Humanity is a citizen of Ohio, its state of incorporation and its principal place of business. Ohio is its principal place of business because its corporate headquarters are located there. Therefore, the adverse parties are of diverse citizenship and since the plaintiff is seeking $1 million in damages, the jurisdictional amount in controversy requirement of §1332(a) is met. Thus, there is diversity-based subject matter jurisdiction over this claim under §1332(a). However, in *Exxon Mobil*, the Supreme Court adhered to the complete diversity rule in a multi-party case and said that if any plaintiff is nondiverse from any defendant, that contaminates the diversity between other adverse parties and there can be no diversity-based original jurisdiction in the lawsuit. And here, plaintiff Hammer, like defendant Humanity, is a citizen of Ohio. Thus, the presence of this nondiverse plaintiff destroys complete diversity, which means that it contaminates the diversity between Diamond and Humanity and precludes the use of §1332 as the basis for original jurisdiction over the state law claim by Diamond against Humanity. This compels us to consider whether the court can exercise supplemental jurisdiction over this state law claim.

6. Subject matter jurisdiction — supplemental jurisdiction   Since the plaintiff Hammer has asserted a federal question claim against defendant Humanity, we must inquire into whether the court can exercise §1367 supplemental jurisdiction over the nondiverse state law claim between Diamond and Humanity. The question, then, under §1367(a), is whether the federal claim by Hammer and the state claim by Diamond can be said to be part of the same constitutional "case," i.e., whether or not they arise out of a common nucleus of operative fact. The federal claim alleges that the workplace maintained by Humanity was unsafe, while Diamond's claim alleges a breach of contract. Since these two claims do not arise out of a common nucleus of operative fact, the court cannot exercise supplemental jurisdiction over this state law claim by Diamond against Humanity. Thus, the court cannot exercise subject matter jurisdiction over this claim.

7. Venue   Assuming the court had subject matter jurisdiction over the claim, which we have determined it did not, we would look to see if venue in Indiana was proper. Since the lawsuit contains a federal question claim, the proper statutory basis for the assessment of venue of all claims in the suit is §1391(b) because subject matter jurisdiction is not founded solely upon diversity. Under §1391(b), this claim can be brought in the Indiana federal court because under §1391(b)(1), it is a state where the defendant resides. The defendant resides in Indiana for venue purposes because, under §1391(c), it is subject to personal jurisdiction in this one-district state.

II. Jack v. Humanity

1. Choice of law — jurisdictional statute   Under Rule 4(k)(1), since there is no applicable federal jurisdictional statute, we look to the long-arm statute of the forum state to determine if there is a statutory basis for personal jurisdiction.

2. Statutory basis for personal jurisdiction   The answer here is the same as was given in connection with Diamond's claim against Humanity. Although Humanity's operations seem to be centered around Ohio, they did negotiate an agreement with Diamond, a company whose headquarters are located in Indiana. The contract was conducted through an exchange of email and fax transmissions that were sent to and from Humanity's executive offices in Indiana. There were also three phone conversations that Humanity employees in Ohio had with Diamond supervisors in Indiana concerning how to perform their job and on one occasion, a Humanity employee had to meet with Diamond supervisors in Indiana to solve a problem. All of these facts indicate that Humanity met the statutory requirement of "transacting business within the state" as contained in the Indiana long-arm statute. Even though none of these activities relates to the unsafe workplace and breach of contract claims that Jack filed against Humanity, this does not detract from the fact that Humanity has non-Jack-related contacts that satisfy the state long-arm statute.

There is no evidence that any other provision of the long-arm statute applies to Humanity. But satisfying one provision is sufficient.

3. Constitutionality of personal jurisdiction   Having determined the existence of statutory jurisdiction, we now must determine whether the exercise of that jurisdiction is consistent with the due process requirements of the Fourteenth Amendment.

The first portion of this test is the *International Shoe* contacts inquiry. This is a twofold inquiry. First, to what extent, if at all, did the defendant create and maintain a purposeful relationship with the forum state? Second, is the court seeking to exert general or specific jurisdiction?

Here, the answer concerning extent of contacts is the same as was provided in the context of the Diamond claim against Humanity. The fact that these contacts are unrelated to Jack's claim against Humanity does not change the fact of these contacts, although it certainly is relevant to determining whether the court is being asked to exercise specific or general jurisdiction. Although Humanity's operations seem to be centered around Ohio, they did negotiate an agreement with Diamond, a company whose headquarters are located in Indiana. The contract was conducted through an exchange of email and fax transmissions that were sent to and from Humanity's executive offices in Indiana. There were also three phone conversations that Humanity employees in Ohio had with Diamond supervisors in Indiana concerning how to perform their job and on one occasion a Humanity employee had to meet with Diamond supervisors in Indiana to solve a problem. All of these facts indicate that Humanity has purposefully availed itself of the benefits and protections of Indiana law and that these contacts are more than isolated.

With respect to the second portion of the *International Shoe* contacts assessment, the court is being asked to exercise general jurisdiction since Jack's claims against Humanity concern the safety of the workplace in Ohio and the breach of his employment contract in Ohio. Neither of these claims arise out of Humanity's activities in the forum state of Indiana.

Since the court is being asked to assert general jurisdiction, a higher threshold of contacts is needed to meet the *International Shoe* test than if it were being asked to exercise specific jurisdiction. Nevertheless, the affiliating relationship between Humanity and Indiana in the form of the contacts undertaken to negotiate and implement the contract could be viewed as sufficiently extensive to meet the *Shoe* test for constitutionality for general jurisdiction, although it probably would be a close call.

The second portion of the constitutional test is the application of the "fairness factors" outlined in *Volkswagen*. The plaintiff has little or no interest in an Indiana forum since it is not a forum citizen. The forum state has little or no interest in providing a forum for the enforcement of contracts entered into by two noncitizens. The interstate judicial system has little if any efficiency interest in Indiana as the forum since all of the evidence would be found in Ohio. Therefore, in light of the fact that the *International Shoe* analysis resulted in a close call, the *Volkswagen* fairness factors push the decision in the direction of denying the exercise of personal jurisdiction over Humanity. On the other hand, it certainly can be argued that since personal jurisdiction exists over Humanity already with respect to the claim by Diamond, there is little if any additional inconvenience of a constitutional magnitude associated with subjecting Humanity to the exercise of power over it in connection with Jack's claims. But also note that if, as concluded, the court will not have subject matter jurisdiction over Diamond's claim against Humanity, then there would be no reason to permit the exercise of personal jurisdiction over Humanity in connection with Jack's claims.

4. Subject matter jurisdiction — federal question   Jack's first claim is a federal statutory claim brought under the OSHA and therefore falls within the court's federal question subject matter jurisdiction under 28 U.S.C. §1331. There is no jurisdictional amount in controversy requirement under §1331 so the fact that the claim is for $50,000 is irrelevant.

5. Subject matter jurisdiction — diversity of citizenship   Jack is a citizen of Ohio. Under the definition of corporate citizenship for diversity jurisdiction purposes found in 28 U.S.C. §1332(c), Humanity is a citizen of Ohio, its state of incorporation and its principal place of business. Ohio is its principal place of business because its corporate headquarters are located there. This means that the parties are not of diverse citizenship and since Jack's second claim for breach of his employment contract is brought under state law, there is no subject matter jurisdiction over this claim under either §1331 or §1332.

6. *Subject matter jurisdiction — supplemental jurisdiction* Can the federal court exercise supplemental jurisdiction over this breach of contract claim under 28 U.S.C. §1367? Under §1367(a), if the contract claim is deemed part of the same case as a federal claim, then supplemental jurisdiction can be exercised. Jack has a federal question claim but it is for violation of a law requiring a safe environment and the contract claim is for failure to pay his wages. These two claims do not arise out of a common nucleus of operative fact and, therefore, supplemental jurisdiction under §1367 is unavailable.

7. *Venue* Under §1391(b), venue for the federal claim would lie in the Indiana federal court because under §1391(b)(1), it is a state where the defendant, Humanity, resides. The defendant resides in Indiana for venue purposes because, under §1391(c), it is subject to personal jurisdiction in this one-district state. If the court exercises supplemental jurisdiction over the state law claim, most courts hold that supplemental claims do not need to meet the statutory venue requirement. But in those jurisdictions that take the contrary view, venue would lie over this state law claim also under §1391(b)(1) for the same reason mentioned in connection with the federal question claim.

8. *Joinder of parties* Under Fed. R. Civ. P. 20, multiple plaintiffs can join in one action if they meet two requirements: (1) they assert claims that arise out of the same transaction or occurrence; and (2) there is a single question of law or fact common to their claims. Diamond's claim against Humanity is for failure to pay its monthly fee. Jack's claim against Humanity is for failure to maintain a safe workplace and failure to pay his salary. These claims do not arise out of the same transaction and thus joinder of the second plaintiff is improper under Rule 20 and that party will be dismissed.

III. Humanity v. BancOhio

1. *Statutory basis for personal jurisdiction* BancOhio is an Ohio corporation whose only branch is in Ohio. There is no evidence that BancOhio has any business dealings with anyone in Indiana and there is no allegation of any tortious conduct on its part. Consequently, there is no statutory basis for the exercise of personal jurisdiction over it in Indiana. Thus, it is unnecessary to undertake a constitutional inquiry concerning personal jurisdiction.

2. *Subject matter jurisdiction — diversity of citizenship* Humanity's claim is for indemnity in connection with the claims against it by Jack and Diamond. This is a state law claim. Humanity is a citizen of Ohio, its state of incorporation and its principal place of business. BancOhio is also a citizen of Ohio. Therefore there is no §1332(a) diversity jurisdiction over this claim.

3. *Subject matter jurisdiction — supplemental jurisdiction* Since this third-party claim is a nondiverse state law claim, can the court exercise supplemental

jurisdiction over this claim under §1367? This indemnity claim, because of the nature of an indemnity claim, is part of the same case as Diamond's breach of contract claim against Humanity. But since it would not be viewed as part of the same case as Jack's federal OSHA claim, since these two claims do not arise out of a common nucleus of fact, the federal claim cannot be the anchor for asserting supplemental jurisdiction over this indemnity claim under §1367(a). Moreover, since the plaintiff Hammer destroyed complete diversity between the adverse parties, under *Exxon Mobil*, there is no diversity-based original jurisdiction over Diamond's state law claim against Humanity. Thus, since this claim does not fall within the court's original jurisdiction, it cannot be the anchor for exercising supplemental jurisdiction over the indemnity claim. So the court cannot exercise supplemental jurisdiction over this indemnity claim.

Humanity's separate claim for damage to its reputation is another state law tort claim. There is no diversity and so the question is whether the court can exercise supplemental jurisdiction over this claim under §1367. This claim for damage to its reputation caused by failure to process Humanity's checks to Diamond and Jack is part of the same case as Diamond's diversity-based state law breach of contract claim against Humanity. But, just as discussed in connection with the indemnity claim, per the ruling in *Exxon Mobil*, that breach of contract claim does not fall within the court's original jurisdiction and so there is no claim with original jurisdiction to be used as the basis for exercising supplemental jurisdiction over this state law claim.

4. Venue   Since there is no basis for subject matter jurisdiction over these claims there is no reason to discuss venue.

5. Joinder of claims   This indemnity claim is joinable under Rule 14(a). The tort claim for injury to reputation, however, is not joinable under Rule 14(a). But since the indemnity claim is joinable under Rule 14(a), this additional claim is joinable under Rule 18, which provides for unlimited joinder for multiple claims by one party against another.

6. Joinder of parties   BancOhio, a third-party defendant, is joinable under Rule 14(a).

IV. Humanity v. Diamond

1. Statutory basis for personal jurisdiction   Diamond, by filing the original complaint, has consented to the exercise of personal jurisdiction over it.

2. Constitutionality of personal jurisdiction   Diamond, by filing the original complaint, has consented to the exercise of personal jurisdiction over it.

3. Subject matter jurisdiction — definition of corporate citizenship   Diamond, under §1332(c), is a citizen of Delaware, its state of incorporation, and Indiana, the state of its principal place of business. Its principal place of business is in Indiana because though it manages operations in New York, Connecticut, and Ohio, its corporate headquarters are in Indiana. Humanity is a citizen of Ohio.

4. Subject matter jurisdiction — diversity of citizenship   This is a state law tort counterclaim seeking damages in the amount of $50,000. Diamond, under §1332(c), is a citizen of Delaware, its state of incorporation, and Indiana, the state of its principal place of business. Its principal place of business is in Indiana because though it manages operations in New York, Connecticut, and Ohio, its corporate headquarters are in Indiana. Humanity is a citizen of Ohio. Therefore the parties are of diverse citizenship. But the amount in controversy, $50,000, does not meet the "in excess of $75,000" requirement of §1332(a). Thus, there is no diversity jurisdiction.

5. Subject matter jurisdiction — supplemental jurisdiction   Humanity's counterclaim alleges a breach of the contract that is the subject of the plaintiff Diamond's complaint against Humanity. Therefore, it would be deemed part of the same case as Diamond's state law claim. Ordinarily, therefore, this compulsory counterclaim would fall within the court's supplemental jurisdiction under §1367(a). But though Humanity and Diamond are diverse, we already concluded that the presence of the nondiverse plaintiff Hammer destroyed complete diversity, which removed §1332 as a basis for original jurisdiction over Diamond's claim against Humanity. And since we also determined that Diamond's state law claim would not fall within the court's supplemental jurisdiction, then there would be no subject matter jurisdiction over that claim and, therefore, none over this otherwise compulsory counterclaim.

6. Venue   Since the court cannot exercise subject matter jurisdiction over this claim, there is no need to discuss venue. Moreover, since this is not a claim by a plaintiff, the venue statute does not need to be considered since venue rules only apply to claims by plaintiffs.

7. Joinder of claims   Under Rule 13(a), all counterclaims are joinable.

QUESTION #2

I. Diamond and Jack Hammer v. Humanity

1. Removal   Since this suit was filed in Indiana state court, the first step would be to remove the case to a federal court in Indiana. This is governed by §1441, and §1441 only permits removal to the federal court located in the state where the state court is located.

Diamond's state law tort claim is not removable under §1441(a) because, per *Exxon Mobil*, the court cannot exercise diversity-based original jurisdiction over it. Since we also have determined that this claim would not fall within the court's supplemental jurisdiction, it is nonremovable.

Jack's federal claim is removable under §1441(a).

Jack's nondiverse state law claim against Humanity is not removable because it does not fall within the federal court's original or supplemental jurisdiction. The question then becomes whether this otherwise nonremovable claim can be removed pursuant to §1441(c). To do that, it has to be separate and independent from Jack's removable federal claim. Jack's federal question claim alleges a violation of a law requiring a safe environment while the state law claim alleges a breach of the contractual duty to pay his wages. These two claims are separate and independent since the resolution of one would not affect the disposition of the other. Consequently, the state law claim can be removed pursuant to §1441(c). That section does give the federal court the discretion to remove the federal claim and remand the state law claim if the latter predominates.

2. Transfer   Having determined that Jack's claims can be removed to federal court in Indiana, the next question is whether the plaintiff could successfully move the federal court to transfer the case to the federal court in Ohio under 28 U.S.C. §1404.

Section 1404 permits transfer in the interests of convenience and justice to a district court in which the action could have been brought. This means that we have to determine whether the Ohio court would have personal jurisdiction over the defendant Humanity and whether venue would lie in Ohio over Jack's claims against Humanity.

There is no problem with personal jurisdiction over the defendant Humanity in Ohio since it is a citizen of Ohio.

There is no problem with venue over the claims in Ohio because the defendant Humanity is subject to personal jurisdiction there and so venue would lie under §1391(b)(1).

With respect to the convenience inquiry, all of the evidence concerning Jack's claims is in Ohio, as is the defendant itself. This is a sufficient basis for transfer.

QUESTION# 3

I. Humanity v. BancOhio

1. Claim preclusion   BancOhio is seeking to dismiss the entire claim on the ground that this was part of the case that was previously litigated between these two parties in the indemnity action. BancOhio is seeking to invoke the doctrine of claim preclusion. The requirements for doing so are (1) the parties are the same; (2) the cause of action is the same; and (3) there was a final and valid adjudication on the merits of that cause of action.

The parties are the same. Is this reputational tort claim part of the same cause of action that constituted the prior case? Has the plaintiff attempted to split one cause of action into two parts? The courts have defined "cause of action" in this context to mean that if a plaintiff seeks different types of damages for the same wrongful conduct, this constitutes but one claim or cause of action. Here, Humanity alleges that BancOhio's failure to process its checks both entitled it to indemnity on the plaintiffs' claims and damages for injury to its reputation. This constitutes an attempt to seek different types of damage relief for the same wrongful conduct. Thus, the plaintiff has attempted to split one claim. Thus, the requirement that the parties and the cause of action be the same have been met here.

The remaining issue is whether there was a final, valid adjudication on the merits. There was. Thus, the claim will be dismissed.

Since Humanity's claim against BancOhio will be dismissed, there is no reason to resolve whether or not Bank Ohio could have relitigated its defense to that claim on the ground that it used that defense in the indemnity suit.

2. Issue preclusion   If Humanity's claim had not been dismissed, since Humanity is seeking to preclude BancOhio from relitigating the issue of its negligence, it would be seeking to invoke the doctrine of issue preclusion (collateral estoppel) based on the decision in the prior case between these same two parties. Since the same two parties are involved in both cases, there is mutuality of estoppel and so this is not an instance of non-mutual estoppel. The issues to be determined are (1) was this same issue already decided in the prior case; (2) do we know how it was decided; and (3) was its decision necessary to the judgment in the prior case? If all three questions result in a positive answer, then the court will invoke issue preclusion against BancOhio.

In the indemnity action, Humanity claimed that BancOhio was negligent in processing its checks. This is the same issue that Humanity is seeking to preclude relitigation of in the second suit. Since Humanity won its indemnity claim, that judgment must have been based on a finding of the bank's negligence. So the issue was litigated and we know how it was resolved. And the decision on that issue was necessary to the judgment because if the issue had been decided the opposite way, the result would have changed, i.e., Humanity would have lost. Thus, all three requirements for issue preclusion have been met and BancOhio will be precluded from relitigating that issue.

CIVIL PROCEDURE ESSAY EXAM #4

QUESTION #1

I. Band v. Iggy Poop

1. Choice of law — jurisdictional statute   Pursuant to Fed. R. Civ. P. 4(k)(1), in the absence of any applicable federal jurisdictional statute, we look to the state jurisdictional statute of the forum state to determine the statutory validity of exercising personal jurisdiction in New York over the defendant.

2. Statutory basis for personal jurisdiction   Iggy is a citizen of California who downloaded files from a server maintained by a California company, Nerdster. This server is accessible by users in every state, including, therefore, New York. Did Iggy "commit a tortious act" within New York? If this statute is construed to mean that the negligent act had to occur in New York, the answer is no because Iggy's wrongful conduct was in making his version of the band's CD available to other users of the Nerdster network and allowing it to be accessed by users across the country, including New York. So his affirmative actions occurred where he or the Nerdster server is located, and both are located in California. However, the statute could be construed to require only that the injury occur in the forum state. The injury to the band was the loss in sales of its CD. The CD is distributed throughout the country and it stands to reason that a significant portion of those sales occur in the populous state of New York. Thus, a not insignificant amount of revenue loss occurred in New York. Under the injury-based construction of "commits a tortious act," the statute would apply.

Iggy did not transact business in New York. To the extent that New Yorkers retrieved the file he uploaded, this is not affirmative conduct on his part and, in any event, would not be considered transacting "business" since he did not receive anything in return from those who downloaded his file. But if he is deemed to have committed a tortious act in the forum state, then compliance with this provision of the long-arm statute is enough to establish a statutory basis for personal jurisdiction.

Having determined, however, that the tortious act provision of the long-arm statute applies, we now must determine whether the exercise of that jurisdiction is consistent with the due process requirements of the Fourteenth Amendment.

3. Constitutionality of personal jurisdiction   The first portion of the constitutional inquiry is the *International Shoe* contacts inquiry. This is a twofold assessment. First, to what extent, if at all, did the defendant create and maintain a purposeful relationship with the forum state? Second, is the court seeking to exert general or specific jurisdiction?

The *International Shoe* test requires that the defendant Iggy have taken some affirmative step on his part to purposefully create a relationship with New York. His interaction with a web network created in California that is also accessible by other users in New York would not constitute direct action on *his* part to constitute a relationship with the forum state. However, this case should be analyzed under the stream of commerce standard set forth by the Supreme Court in *Asahi*. Under the view articulated by the Justice O'Connor plurality, a participant in a chain of commerce that puts something in the stream of commerce and does something to direct its flow into the forum state is deemed to have created a purposeful relationship with the forum state. Under this view, Iggy put the music in the stream but did nothing to direct it to New York or anywhere else. Under this test, therefore, Iggy would not be said to have created a purposeful relationship with the forum state. Under Justice Brennan's formulation of the stream of commerce test in *Asahi*, however, all that is necessary is that the defendant put the product in the stream and that it ultimately arrives in the forum and causes injury, even if the taking of it to the forum is outside of the defendant's control. Under that analysis, Iggy would have created the necessary relationship with the forum.

Alternatively, one could apply the "effects" test used in intentional tort cases as articulated by the Supreme Court in *Calder v. Jones*. In *Calder*, the plaintiff in a defamation action brought suit in her home state alleging that the distribution of a defamatory article in a periodical had a particularly damaging effect in her home state. Thus, the Court held, because the extraterritorial actions of the author and editor of the defamatory article had a foreseeable, damaging effect on the plaintiff in the forum state (because she both lived and worked in that state), jurisdiction was proper because the defendant's conduct was calculated to injure her in the forum state. While the band does sell a lot of music in New York, it was probably not foreseeable to Iggy that the economic damage to the band would be particularly strongly felt in New York. Thus, *Calder* is distinguishable and inapplicable.

Assuming, therefore, that we conclude, under the Brennan analysis in *Asahi*, that Iggy had a relationship with the forum state, what is the extent of that relationship? The relationship is based on making a file on his computer accessible to downloading by others through the Nerdster network. Although Iggy downloaded 150 songs from the network, the facts indicate that he only made one CD available though the network. This would suggest that his contact with New York is relatively infrequent.

With respect to the second portion of the *International Shoe* contacts assessment, the court is being asked to exercise specific jurisdiction since the band's claim arises out of the conduct (using the Nerdster network) that formed the basis of its cause of action. When the court is exercising specific jurisdiction, a lower threshold of contact is required. Even the limited amount of contact between Iggy and New York would suffice.

The second portion of the constitutional test is the application of the "fairness factors" outlined in *Volkswagen*. Since the plaintiffs are not forum citizens, they have no particular interest in suing in New York. The forum state has little interest in providing this California band with a forum to enforce its pecuniary interests, although it might have an interest in regulating use of the Internet by its citizens. The interstate judicial system has no efficiency interest in New York since none of the evidence or witnesses are located there. In light of the limited extent of the defendant's relationship with the forum, the *Volkswagen* fairness factors tilt the balance against the exercise of personal jurisdiction over Iggy in New York.

4. Subject matter jurisdiction — federal question The band's first claim is a federal claim under the copyright act and, therefore, jurisdiction is found under either 28 U.S.C. §1331 or §1338. There is no jurisdictional amount in controversy requirement under §1331 so the fact that the claim is for $50,000 is irrelevant.

5. Subject matter jurisdiction — diversity of citizenship The band's second claim for tortious interference is a state law claim. The band members are all citizens of California, the state of their permanent domicile since the facts indicate that they were born and raised in California. Iggy is also a citizen of California. Therefore, the parties are not diverse and jurisdiction cannot be based on §1332.

6. Subject matter jurisdiction — supplemental jurisdiction Can the court exercise supplemental jurisdiction under §1367? There is a federal question claim and so the issue is decided under §1367(a). Is the state claim part of the same "case" as the federal claim? This is resolved by determining whether they arise out of a common nucleus of operative fact. Both of these claims are based on Iggy's stealing of their music and so they are part of the same case. The court can exercise supplemental jurisdiction. Under §1367(c), the federal court would have the discretion not to exercise supplemental jurisdiction over the state claim if it raised novel issues of state law, predominated over the federal question, or created the potential for jury confusion. None of these factors appear present in this case. Therefore, the court would exercise supplemental jurisdiction over this nondiverse state law claim.

7. Venue Since there is a federal question claim in this case, subject matter jurisdiction in this civil action is not based solely on diversity. Thus, when assessing venue, each claim brought by a plaintiff must be evaluated under the provision of §1391(b). With respect to both the federal question and supplemental claim filed by the boys, did a substantial part of the underlying events occur in New York? No, and therefore no venue under §1391(b)(2). Does the defendant Iggy reside in New York? No, and therefore no venue under §1391(b)(1). Section 1391(b)(3) is inapplicable because venue is available in California. Therefore, venue does not lie over these claims in New York.

8. Joinder of claims Under Rule 18, a plaintiff can bring multiple claims against a single defendant without limitation. So the second claim is joinable.

9. Joinder of parties Under Fed. R. Civ. P. 20, multiple plaintiffs can join in one action if they meet two requirements: (1) they assert claims that arise out of the same transaction or occurrence; and (2) there is a single question of law or fact common to their claims. The claims of all band members arise out of the same action by the defendant and the question of whether he stole their music is common to all of their claims. So all four plaintiffs can join in this action.

II. Band v. Capitol

1. Statutory basis for personal jurisdiction Although Capitol is a citizen of California, it clearly is doing business in New York. It generates 25% of all of its sales in New York. There is a statutory basis for personal jurisdiction over Capitol in New York.

2. Constitutionality of personal jurisdiction The first portion of this test is the *International Shoe* contacts inquiry. This is a twofold inquiry. First, to what extent, if at all, did the defendant create and maintain a purposeful relationship with the forum state? Second, is the court seeking to exert general or specific jurisdiction? Capitol clearly has a systematic and continuous relationship with New York in light of the extent of its sales in that state.

The band's claim against Capitol is for failure to promote its CD. Since New York is an important market for Capitol, some of that failure clearly occurred in New York. Thus, the court is being asked to exercise specific jurisdiction over Capitol since the band's claim arises, in part at least, out of the defendant's forum activities. But whether the court was exercising specific or general jurisdiction, the continuous nature of the defendant's forum conduct is a sufficient basis for satisfying the "contacts" portion of the constitutional test for jurisdiction.

The second portion of the constitutional test is the application of the "fairness factors" outlined in *Volkswagen*. Since the plaintiffs are not forum citizens, they have no particular interest in suing in New York. The forum state has little interest in providing this California band with a forum to enforce its pecuniary interests, although it might have an interest in regulating the conduct of a major music marketer in its territory. The interstate judicial system has no efficiency interest in New York since none of the evidence or witnesses are located there. But because of the defendant's extensive relationship with the forum state, these fairness factors will not overwhelm the contacts analysis. Jurisdiction is constitutionally permissible over Capitol in New York.

3. Subject matter jurisdiction — diversity of citizenship The band's claim against Capitol is a state law claim. Both the band members and Capitol are citizens of California. (The fact that Capitol is also a citizen of Delaware, its state of incorporation, is irrelevant.) Thus, there is no diversity of citizenship jurisdiction over this state law claim.

4. Subject matter jurisdiction — supplemental jurisdiction Since the band's claim against Capitol is a nondiverse state law claim, can the court exercise supplemental jurisdiction under §1367? The band has a federal claim against Iggy. The question then becomes is the claim against Capitol part of the same case as the claim against Iggy. Do these two claims arise out of a common nucleus of operative fact? The answer is no because the band claims that Iggy stole their music by distributing it over the Internet while they claim that Capitol did not properly market their product. Therefore, the court cannot exercise supplemental jurisdiction under §1367.

5. Venue Since there is no jurisdiction over the claim, there is no need to investigate venue.

6. Joinder of parties Under Fed. R. Civ. P. 20, multiple defendants can be joined in one action if they meet two requirements: (1) the claims asserted against them arise out of the same transaction or occurrence; and (2) there is a single question of law or fact common to these claims. The band's claims against Iggy arise out of his distribution of their music over the Internet. The band's claims against Capitol concern its inadequate marketing. Thus, the claims do not arise out of the same transaction or occurrence and so joinder is improper.

III. Iggy Poop v. Nerdster

1. Statutory basis for personal jurisdiction   Nerdster is transacting business in New York since users of its network come from all states, including New York.

Nerdster is committing a tortious act in New York by causing damage to the band's pecuniary interests in that state as a result of damaging the sales of their music in that state.

Having determined that the long-arm statute applies, we now must determine whether the exercise of that jurisdiction is consistent with the due process requirements of the Fourteenth Amendment.

2. Constitutionality of personal jurisdiction   The first portion of this test is the *International Shoe* contacts inquiry. This is a twofold inquiry. First, to what extent, if at all, did the defendant create and maintain a purposeful relationship with the forum state? Second, is the court seeking to exert general or specific jurisdiction?

The cases addressing the constitutionality of exercising jurisdiction over entities that do business over the Internet focus on the level of interactivity of the defendant's web presence. Nerdster's network encourages individuals to swap files by uploading files onto and downloading files from its server. It has 3 million users from across the country, including New York State. This is a highly interactive site and would meet the constitutional test for creating contacts in the forum state. This is a continuous and systematic relationship with the forum state.

Since both of Iggy's third-party claims against Nerdster arise out of this web activity, the court is being asked to exercise specific jurisdiction. But even if this is viewed as an attempt to exercise general jurisdiction, the level of Nerdster's activity in New York would meet the first part of the constitutional standard.

The second portion of the constitutional test is the application of the "fairness factors" outlined in *Volkswagen*. Since the plaintiff is not a forum citizen he would have no particular interest in suing in New York. The forum state has little interest in providing this California techie with a forum to enforce his interests, although it might have an interest in regulating use of the Internet by its citizens. The interstate judicial system has no efficiency interest in New York since none of the evidence or witnesses are located there. But in light of the extensive relationship between Nerdster and New York, the *Volkswagen* fairness factors would not tilt the balance against the exercise of personal jurisdiction over Iggy in New York. Jurisdiction is proper over Nerdster in New York.

3. Subject matter jurisdiction — diversity of citizenship   Both of Iggy's third-party claims against Nerdster are state law claims. Iggy is a citizen of California and Nerdster, under §1332(c), is a citizen of Delaware, its state of incorporation, and California, the state of its principal place of business, because its headquarters are located in that state. Thus, the parties are not diverse.

4. Subject matter jurisdiction — supplemental jurisdiction   Since the adverse parties to these third-party claims are not diverse and the claim arises under state law, can the court exercise supplemental jurisdiction under §1367? Iggy's first third-party claim is an indemnity claim seeking indemnity for any recovery obtained by the boys against him, including for the federal question claim. Since he is seeking, *inter alia*, indemnity for liability to the plaintiff band members under the federal question claim, this nondiverse state law claim forms part of the same "case" as the federal question claim and therefore meets the requirement of §1367(a) for the exercise of supplemental jurisdiction. Under §1367(c), the federal court would have the discretion not to exercise supplemental jurisdiction over the state claim if it raised novel issues of state law, predominated over the federal question, or created the potential for jury confusion. None of these factors appear present in this case. Therefore, the court would exercise supplemental jurisdiction over this nondiverse state law indemnity claim.

Iggy's second claim is a tort claim for damage to his computer. This claim does not arise from the nucleus of operative fact that gave rise to either the federal question or supplemental claim asserted by the plaintiff band members against Iggy and, therefore, is not part of the same "case" as those claims. Thus, the court could not exercise supplemental jurisdiction over this claim.

5. Venue   The requirements of the venue statute only apply to claims brought by plaintiffs since it refers to where a civil action may "be brought." Plaintiffs bring civil actions and so the venue requirements do not apply to third-party claims.

6. Joinder of claims   Iggy's indemnity claim is joinable as a third-party complaint for indemnity under Rule 14(a). The second claim is not joinable under Rule 14 since it is not for indemnity. But since the indemnity claim is joinable, the other claim becomes joinable under Rule 18, which permits a party with one joinable claim to add an infinite number of other claims.

7. Joinder of parties   Nerdster is joinable under Rule 14(a).

IV. Iggy Poop v. Capitol

1. Statutory basis for personal jurisdiction   Personal jurisdiction over Capitol has already been determined to exist in connection with the plaintiff's claims against Capitol.

2. Constitutionality of personal jurisdiction   Personal jurisdiction over Capitol has already been determined to exist in connection with the plaintiff's claims against Capitol.

3. Subject matter jurisdiction — federal question   This is a federal antitrust law claim so jurisdiction exists under §1331 and §1337.

4. Venue   The requirements of the venue statute only apply to claims brought by plaintiffs since it refers to where a civil action may "be brought." Plaintiffs bring civil actions and so the venue requirements do not apply to cross-claims filed by a party defendant, as here.

5. Joinder of claims   This is a cross-claim. Rule 13(g) governs the joinability of cross-claims. Cross-claims are only joinable if they are transactionally related to the claims in the original complaint. These antitrust claims concerning Capitol's pricing policies have nothing to do with the band's claims against Iggy or Capitol. Consequently, the cross-claim is not joinable.

QUESTION #2

I. Band v. Capitol and Iggy

1. Removal   Since this suit was filed in New York state court, the first step would be to remove the case to a federal court in New York. This is governed by §1441, and §1441 only permits removal to the federal court located in the state where the state court is located. If the case is removable, then the plaintiff will attempt to transfer it to California under §1404.

The band has two claims against Iggy. One is a federal question claim and so it is removable under §1441(a). The second claim falls within the court's supplemental jurisdiction and so it is removable under §1441(a) to the district where the state court is located.

The band's claim against Capitol is a nondiverse state law claim that does not fall within the court's supplemental jurisdiction. Therefore, it is not removable under §1441(a). But an otherwise nonremovable claim can be removed under §1441(c) if it is separate and independent from a federal law claim. The breach of contract claim against Capitol for not adequately promoting the band's music is separate and independent from both its copyright and tortious interference claims against Iggy since the disposition of the band's claims against Iggy will have no effect on the disposition of their claim against Capitol. Thus, this requirement of §1441(c) is met. That section does give the federal court the discretion to remove the federal claim and remand the state law claim if the latter predominates. But that is not the case here.

QUESTION #3(a)

I. Iggy v. Band

1. Claim preclusion/res judicata   The band would be attempting to preclude Iggy from asserting that claim under the doctrine of claim preclusion. The doctrine of claim preclusion applies if Iggy's claim against the band is deemed to be a compulsory counterclaim to their claims against him in the original suit. The test for whether or not a counterclaim is compulsory in federal court is found in Rule 13(a), which defines compulsory counterclaims as claims that are transactionally related to the plaintiff's claim. This test is clearly met here since Iggy's claim for damage to his reputation alleges that the filing of the band's claims against him caused the damage. Thus, the claims are related and his claim would be precluded.

QUESTION #3(b)

I. Jay Cool v. Iggy

1. Issue preclusion/collateral estoppel   Since Iggy is only attempting to preclude relitigation of a single issue, his violation of the copyright act, he is attempting to invoke the doctrine of issue preclusion (collateral estoppel). But he is attempting to invoke it against a party that was not a party to the original action. This is prohibited by the Due Process Clause. One can never invoke issue preclusion against a stranger to the original lawsuit.

CIVIL PROCEDURE ESSAY EXAM #5

QUESTION #1

I. Spouses v. BB

1. Choice of law — jurisdictional statute   Pursuant to Fed. R. Civ. P. 4(k)(1), in the absence of an applicable federal jurisdictional statute, we look to the long-arm statute of the forum state to determine whether there is a statutory basis for the exercise of personal jurisdiction.

2. Statutory basis for personal jurisdiction   Did BB commit a tortious act within Louisiana? If the statute is construed to require that the negligent act occurred in Louisiana, the answer is no since the creation of the record occurred in Pennsylvania or wherever the record was produced and/or written, which certainly was not Louisiana. On the other hand, if the statute is construed to require only that the injury was suffered in Louisiana, then the defendant did "commit a tortious act" within Louisiana.

Did BB "transact business" within Louisiana? Yes. BB was in New Orleans for one concert, even though he was only there for less than one full day. So he did transact business in the state. The statute also covers the acts of agents transacting business. If MCI is viewed as his agent, it distributed and probably promoted his record in Louisiana.

Having concluded that the long-arm statute applies, we now must determine whether the exercise of that jurisdiction is consistent with the due process requirements of the Fourteenth Amendment.

3. Constitutionality of personal jurisdiction   The first portion of this test is the *International Shoe* contacts inquiry. This is a twofold inquiry. First, to what extent, if at all, did the defendant create and maintain a purposeful relationship with the forum state? Second, is the court seeking to exert general or specific jurisdiction?

BB clearly has a purposeful relationship with Louisiana through his performance of a concert in Louisiana. But since he was only there for less than one day, this is an isolated occurrence. But if you also consider the distribution of his CDs nationwide by MCI, then he is a part of a chain of commerce and we need to invoke the "stream of commerce" standard set out by the Court in *Asahi*. The O'Connor plurality opinion provides that the defendant must not only put the product in the stream of commerce but unilaterally do something to direct it to the forum state. While BB put his song in the stream, he did nothing to market or otherwise direct it to Louisiana. That conduct was undertaken by MCI. Thus, under the O'Connor analysis, the stream of commerce test would not be satisfied. Under the analysis offered by the Brennan group of four Justices in *Asahi*, it is sufficient if the defendant put the product in the stream and it was taken into the forum by a third party and caused injury there. That test would be satisfied here. And under that standard, the stream of products into Louisiana through MCI's distribution chain could be significantly more than isolated.

In either instance, there is some contact. The question then becomes whether the court is being asked to exercise specific or general jurisdiction. Since the plaintiffs' claims arise directly out of BB's contacts with Louisiana in the form of the distribution of his music, the court is being asked to exercise specific jurisdiction. This requires a low threshold of contacts and the test is met here.

Having found that the "contacts" portion of the constitutional test has been met, we must examine the second portion of the constitutional test — the application of the "fairness factors" outlined in *Volkswagen*. The plaintiffs are forum citizens so they have an interest in having the suit heard in Louisiana. For that reason, the forum state has an interest in providing a forum in which its citizens can receive compensation for their injuries. With respect to the interstate judicial system's efficiency interests, lots of the evidence and witnesses are located in Louisiana. So the *Volkswagen* fairness factors further support the exercise of personal jurisdiction over BB in Louisiana.

4. Subject matter jurisdiction — diversity of citizenship   The plaintiffs assert a $1 million tort claim against BB. The plaintiffs are Louisiana citizens because it is the state of their permanent domicile as they are lifelong residents. The defendant is a citizen of Pennsylvania because it is the state of his permanent domicile, since he was born and raised there. Thus, the parties are diverse and the claim meets the jurisdictional amount in controversy requirement, so there is subject matter jurisdiction over this claim under §1332(a).

5. Venue   Because there is no federal question claim asserted in the complaint, subject matter jurisdiction in this civil action is founded solely upon diversity of citizenship. Thus, the venue assessment that must be undertaken for each claim brought by a plaintiff must be made pursuant to the terms of §1391(a). Venue would not lie under §1391(a)(1) because the noncorporate defendant does not reside in Louisiana. Venue would lie under §1391(a)(2) because a substantial part of the events giving rise to the claim — the murder of the police officers — occurred in the chosen district.

6. Joinder of parties plaintiff   Under Fed. R. Civ. P. 20, multiple plaintiffs can join in one action if they meet two requirements: (1) they assert claims that arise out of the same transaction or occurrence; and (2) there is a single question of law or fact common to their claims. The claims of both wives arise out of the same action by the defendant and the question of whether the defendant's music proximately caused the death of their husbands is common to both suits. So the plaintiffs can join in this action.

II. Spouses v. MCI

1. Statutory basis for personal jurisdiction   Does the long-arm statute apply? MCI clearly conducts business in Louisiana. It sponsored the promotional tour that took BB into Louisiana. It markets his music and that of its other artists on an interactive web page, which results in sales in Louisiana.

MCI also can be said to have committed a tortious act in Louisiana. The plaintiffs allege that its distribution and sale of the CD caused the death of their husbands in Louisiana. If the long-arm statute is construed to require that the negligent act occurred in Louisiana, it could be argued that the distribution into Louisiana through the highly interactive web site meets that requirement. Alternatively, if the statute is construed to require only that the injury was suffered in Louisiana, then the defendant also did "commit a tortious act" within Louisiana since the injury was sustained in Louisiana.

2. Constitutionality of personal jurisdiction Having concluded that the long-arm statute applies, we now must determine whether the exercise of that jurisdiction is consistent with the due process requirements of the Fourteenth Amendment. The first portion of this test is the *International Shoe* contacts inquiry. This is a twofold inquiry. First, to what extent, if at all, did the defendant create and maintain a purposeful relationship with the forum state? Second, is the court seeking to exert general or specific jurisdiction?

The cases involving a defendant's use of the Internet for ecommerce conclude that the defendant will be deemed to have created a relationship with the forum state for *International Shoe* "contact" purposes if it has a highly interactive web page. This one is highly interactive since it permits individuals to consummate transactions over the web through purchases with credit cards.

The facts do not indicate the extent of this relationship with Louisiana customers. But whether these sales were isolated or systematic, the court is being asked to exercise specific jurisdiction since the cause of action arises out of those contacts. Thus, the "contacts" portion of the constitutional test is satisfied.

Having found that the "contacts" portion of the constitutional test has been met, we must examine the second portion of the constitutional test — the application of the "fairness factors" outlined in *Volkswagen*. The plaintiffs are forum citizens so they have an interest in having the suit heard in Louisiana. For that reason, the forum state has an interest in providing a forum in which its citizens can receive compensation for their injuries. With respect to the interstate judicial system's efficiency interests, lots of the evidence and witnesses are located in Louisiana. So the *Volkswagen* fairness factors add additional support for the exercise of personal jurisdiction over BB in Louisiana.

3. Subject matter jurisdiction — definition of corporate citizenship Under the definition of corporate citizenship in §1332(c), MCI is a citizen of Delaware, the state of its incorporation, and California, the state of its principal place of business based on the presence of its offices and recording studios there.

4. Subject matter jurisdiction — diversity of citizenship The plaintiffs' claims against MCI are state law tort claims. The plaintiffs are citizens of Louisiana because of their permanent domicile there. Under the definition of corporate citizenship in §1332(c), MCI is a citizen of Delaware, the state of its incorporation, and California, the state of its principal place of business based on the presence of its offices and recording studios there. Thus, all of the adverse parties are of diverse citizenship. The $1 million claim meets the jurisdictional amount in controversy requirement. Thus, there is subject matter jurisdiction over this claim under §1332(a).

5. Venue Venue over this diversity claim is governed by §1391(a). Venue would lie under §1391(a)(1) because the corporate defendant resides in Louisiana. Section 1391(c) provides that a corporation resides for venue purposes in a state if that state can exercise personal jurisdiction over it. Personal jurisdiction can be exercised over MCI in Louisiana. Thus, there is venue under §1391(a)(1). Since Louisiana is a multi-district state, we look to see whether there would be personal jurisdiction over MCI in the area of the Eastern District, i.e., New Orleans. The facts clearly indicate that there would.

Venue also would lie under §1391(a)(2) because a substantial part of the events giving rise to the claim — the murder of the police officers — occurred in the chosen district. Satisfying either of these two portions of §1391(a) is sufficient.

6. Joinder of parties defendant   Multiple defendants can be joined in a single lawsuit if there is asserted against all of them claims that (1) arise out of a common series of occurrences or transactions; and (2) contain one single common question of law or fact. The claims against both BB and MCI arise out of the creation and distribution of BB's music and so the first requirement is met. The second requirement is also met since both claims require an assessment of the extent of damage suffered by the plaintiffs.

III. Spouses v. Tom's Music

1. Statutory basis of personal jurisdiction   Tom's is a citizen of California. Does any portion of the Louisiana long-arm statute provide a basis for jurisdiction over Tom's? There is no evidence that this local New York music store has any dealings of any kind in Louisiana and no evidence of a web site. So the doing business provision of the long-arm statute would not apply. Did Tom's commit a tortious act in Louisiana? Possibly. If it is sufficient that the injury suffered by Tom's allegedly negligent act occurred in the forum state, then there could be an argument that this statute applies. The plaintiffs allege that Tom's negligent sale of music with violent lyrics contributed to the environment that caused the gang members' conduct, which resulted in the murder of the plaintiffs' husbands in the forum state. This should be enough to satisfy the statutory requirement of causing injury in the forum state if the "committing a tortious act" provision is construed to require only the occurrence of the injury in the forum. But if that provision was interpreted also to require that the negligent act occur in the forum state, then the long-arm statute would not apply to Tom's.

2. Constitutional analysis of personal jurisdiction   In the unlikely event that the court found that the long-arm statute applied to Tom's, we would need to undertake a constitutional due process analysis of the exercise of personal jurisdiction over Tom's. The first portion of this test is the *International Shoe* contacts inquiry. This is a twofold inquiry. First, to what extent, if at all, did the defendant create and maintain a purposeful relationship with the forum state? Second, is the court seeking to exert general or specific jurisdiction?

Tom's did not create any relationship with Louisiana, either directly or indirectly, as it was not part of a chain of commerce, but, rather, a retailer at the end of the chain. Thus, without any contacts in Louisiana, there is no need for further analysis. It would be unconstitutional to exercise personal jurisdiction over Tom's in Louisiana.

3. Subject matter jurisdiction — diversity of citizenship   This is a state law tort claim. The plaintiffs are citizens of Louisiana and the defendant is a citizen of California. So the parties are diverse. But each plaintiff is bringing a $50,000 claim against Tom's. Under the non-aggregation rules, multiple plaintiffs cannot aggregate the value of their claims against a common defendant to meet the jurisdictional amount in controversy requirement of §1332. Thus, there is no diversity-based original jurisdiction over this claim under §1332.

4. Subject matter jurisdiction — federal question   The fact that the complaint includes a reference to the First Amendment does not matter since, under the well pleaded complaint rule, the federal question must appear in the plaintiff's prima facie case. This federal issue appears as a response to an anticipated defense by the defendant. Thus, there is no federal question jurisdiction under §1331.

5. Subject matter jurisdiction — supplemental jurisdiction   In the absence of diversity and federal question jurisdiction, can the court exercise supplemental jurisdiction over this nondiverse state law claim? In *Exxon Mobil*, the Court held that where multiple plaintiffs are diverse from a common defendant but the state law claims do not meet the jurisdictional amount in controversy, as long as one diverse plaintiff does have a state law claim that meets that requirement, the other claims can be considered under §1367(b) for the exercise of diversity-based supplemental jurisdiction. Here, the wives do have tort claims against BB that meet the amount in controversy requirement. So that makes the claims by the wives against Tom's subject to §1367(b) supplemental jurisdiction. And since there is no federal question claim in the case, we must look to §1367(b) as the source for supplemental jurisdiction. Section 1367(b) does not permit supplemental jurisdiction over claims by plaintiffs (which this is) against a defendant joined under, *inter alia*, Rule 20. Since Tom's would be a defendant joined under Rule 20, there can be no exercise of supplemental jurisdiction over this claim.

6. Venue   Since there is no subject matter jurisdiction over this claim, it is unnecessary to examine venue.

7. Joinder of parties defendant   Multiple defendants can be joined in a single lawsuit if there is asserted against all of them claims that (1) arise out of a common series of occurrences or transactions; and (2) contain one single common question of law or fact. The claims against BB, MCI, and Tom's arise out of the creation, distribution, and sale of BB's music and so the first requirement is met. The second requirement is also met since all of these claims require an assessment of the extent of damage suffered by the plaintiffs.

IV. MCI v. Joe Brown

1. Statutory basis for personal jurisdiction   Does the long-arm statute apply? Brown has committed a tortious act in Louisiana if the statute is construed to apply when the injury occurs in the forum state. The facts do not suggest that Brown has transacted business in the state.

2. Constitutionality of personal jurisdiction   Is the application of the statute constitutional? If Brown has purposefully created contacts with Louisiana, it could only be through the stream of commerce analysis propounded by Justice Brennan.

Brown did nothing to push the product (the song he wrote) into the Louisiana market. But the injury did occur there and that would be sufficient for the Brennan quartet in *Asahi*.

If we conclude that Brown has contacts, then this is an attempt to exercise specific jurisdiction and even his limited contacts would be sufficient.

Having found that the "contacts" portion of the constitutional test has been met, we must examine the second portion of the constitutional test — the application of the "fairness factors" outlined in *Volkswagen*. The plaintiff is not a forum citizen and so it would not have an interest in having the suit heard in Louisiana. For that reason, the forum state would not have a strong interest in providing a forum in which its citizens can receive compensation for their injuries. With respect to the interstate judicial system's efficiency interests, since MCI is seeking indemnity against Brown, there is a lot of commonality between the issues in this claim and the issues in the claims asserted by the plaintiffs against MCI. So the *Volkswagen* fairness factors are equivocal in this context.

3. Subject matter jurisdiction — diversity of citizenship   The indemnity claim is a state law claim. The parties are diverse since the plaintiffs are Louisiana citizens and Brown is a citizen of California. The amount in controversy requirement is met since the indemnity claim could result in indemnity to the tune of $1 million.

The breach of contract claim seeks only $25,000 and so the jurisdictional amount in controversy requirement of §1332(a) is not independently satisfied. But since a single plaintiff can aggregate the value of multiple claims brought against a single defendant, MCI can aggregate the value of its claims against Brown and this will meet the amount in controversy requirement. Thus, this claim also will fall within §1332 jurisdiction.

4. Venue   The requirements of the venue statute only apply to claims brought by plaintiffs since it refers to where a civil action may "be brought." Plaintiffs bring civil actions and so the venue requirements do not apply to third-party claims filed by a party defendant, as here.

5. Joinder of claims   The indemnity claim against Brown can be joined under Fed. R. Civ. P 14(a) since it is a claim for indemnity. The breach of contract claim does not fall within Rule 14(a) but it can be joined under the terms of Rule 18, which permits a party to join an infinite number of additional claims to a properly joined claim.

V. MCI v. Tom's Music

1. Statutory basis of personal jurisdiction   The answer here mirrors the answer given in connection with the plaintiffs's claim against Tom's. Tom's is a citizen of California. Does any portion of the Louisiana long-arm statute provide a basis for jurisdiction over Tom's? There is no evidence that this local New York music store has any dealings of any kind in Louisiana and no evidence of a web site. So the doing business provision of the long-arm statute would not apply. Did Tom's commit a tortious act in Louisiana? Possibly. If it is sufficient that the injury suffered from Tom's allegedly negligent act occurred in the forum state, then there could be an argument that this statute applies. The plaintiffs allege that Tom's negligent sale of music with violent lyrics contributed to the environment that caused the gang members' conduct, which resulted in the murder of the plaintiffs' husbands in the forum state. This should be enough to satisfy the statutory requirement of causing injury in the forum state if the "committing a tortious act" provision is construed to require only the occurrence of the injury in the forum. But if that provision was interpreted also to require that the negligent act occur in the forum state, then the long-arm statute would not apply to Tom's.

2. Constitutional analysis of personal jurisdiction   The answer here mirrors the answer given in connection with the plaintiffs' claim against Tom's. In the unlikely event that the court found that the long-arm statute applied to Tom's, we would need to undertake a constitutional due process analysis of the exercise of personal jurisdiction over Tom's. The first portion of this test is the *International Shoe* contacts inquiry. This is a twofold inquiry. First, to what extent, if at all, did the defendant create and maintain a purposeful relationship with the forum state? Second, is the court seeking to exert general or specific jurisdiction?

Tom's did not create any relationship with Louisiana, either directly or indirectly, as it was not part of a chain of commerce, but, rather, a retailer at the end of the chain. Thus, without any contacts in Louisiana, there is no need for further analysis. It would be unconstitutional to exercise personal jurisdiction over Tom's in Louisiana.

3. Subject matter jurisdiction — diversity of citizenship   MCI is a citizen of Delaware and California. Tom's is a citizen of California. The parties are nondiverse. Thus, there can be no §1332-based original jurisdiction over this cross-claim.

4. Subject matter jurisdiction — supplemental jurisdiction   Can the court exercise supplemental jurisdiction over this otherwise diverse state law claim that does not meet the amount in controversy requirement? Is it part of the same "case" as the claims brought by the plaintiff? The answer to this is no because this is a breach of contract claim for failure to pay for the CDs and it does not arise out of the nucleus of operative fact that gave rise to the spouse's tort claims. Thus, no supplemental jurisdiction over this claim.

5. Venue   Since there is no jurisdiction over the claim, there is no need to examine venue.

6. Joinder of cross-claim   Rule 13(g) permits joinder of cross-claims only when they are transactionally related to the plaintiffs' claims. This claim for failure to pay for merchandise is not transactionally related to the plaintiffs' tort claims, even though it is failure to pay for BB's CDs. So the claim is not joinable.

QUESTION #2(a)

I. BB v. Spouses

The spouses would be attempting to preclude BB from asserting these claims under the doctrine of claim preclusion. The doctrine of claim preclusion applies if BB's two claims against the spouses in the second action are deemed to constitute compulsory counterclaims to their claims against him in the original suit. The test for whether or not a counterclaim is compulsory in federal court is found in Rule 13(a), which defines compulsory counterclaims as claims that are transactionally related to the plaintiff's claim. The plaintiffs' claims assert that his music caused their husbands' deaths. His claims allege that their public statements during the course of that litigation damaged him. This does not meet the Rule 13(a) test and so the claims would not be precluded.

QUESTION#2(b)

I. Children v. BB

The request by the children is an attempt to invoke the doctrine of issue preclusion (collateral estoppel). But since the children were not a party to the first case, this would be an attempt at non-mutual issue preclusion. And since the children are the plaintiffs in this second suit, this would be an attempt to invoke offensive non-mutual issue preclusion. The Supreme Court in *Parklane* ruled that offensive non-mutual collateral estoppel is generally not permitted when the court concludes either (1) that the plaintiff could easily have joined in the first lawsuit (so as not to encourage "wait and see" plaintiffs) or (2) that invoking issue preclusion would be unfair to the party against whom it is being invoked such as where the defendant did not have incentive to try its best in the first lawsuit. Lack of incentive could occur where the stakes were much lower in the first lawsuit brought against the defendant or where the second suit provides the defendant procedural opportunities that were not available in the first action that could cause a different result.

The children could have joined in the first suit. Under Rule 20, their claims against BB would have qualified them for joinder. Thus, they cannot invoke offensive non-mutual issue preclusion.

The request by BB to prelude litigation on the issue of causation is also an attempt to invoke issue preclusion. But since the children were not parties to the original action, issue preclusion cannot be invoked against them. To do so would violate the Due Process Clause of the Fourteenth Amendment.

CIVIL PROCEDURE ESSAY EXAM #6

QUESTION #1

I. Emillion v. CBI

1. Choice of law — jurisdictional statute Since suit was filed in federal court, in the absence of any federal jurisdictional provision, per Rule 4(k)(1), we look to the state jurisdictional statute of the forum state to determine the statutory sufficiency of personal jurisdiction.

2. Statutory and constitutional basis for personal jurisdiction Defendant CBI is a forum citizen so the state has inherent power to exercise personal jurisdiction over it and we do not need to look to a long-arm statute or the Due Process Clause of the Constitution.

3. Subject matter jurisdiction — federal question Emillion's claim under the federal Hurricane and Flood Restoration Act falls under the court's federal question jurisdiction codified at §1331.

4. Subject matter jurisdiction — diversity of citizenship The plaintiff is a citizen of Louisiana, as his permanent domicile is there. Pursuant to the definition of corporate citizenship in §1332(c), defendant CBI is a citizen of both Delaware, its state of incorporation, and Louisiana, the state of its principal place of business. Thus, these parties are not diverse and so there will be no original §1332-based jurisdiction over Emillion's tort claim against CBI.

5. Subject matter jurisdiction — supplemental jurisdiction Since the plaintiff asserted a §1331 claim against CBI, the question is whether the court can exercise supplemental jurisdiction over the nondiverse state law claim brought by Emillion against CBI under §1367(a). This turns on whether the two claims form part of the same constitutional "case," i.e., whether they arise out of a common nucleus of operative fact. Both the state and federal claims arise out of concerns over the quality of the repair work done on the plaintiff's home by the defendant. So the two claims meet the same case requirement for supplemental jurisdiction. The trial court could decline to exercise supplemental jurisdiction over the state law claim pursuant to the factors set forth in §1367(c) but there is no indication that these factors would favor dismissal because there is no suggestion that the state law claim is novel or complex or is the predominant part of the case.

6. Venue Since there is a federal question asserted by the plaintiff, subject matter jurisdiction over this civil action does not arise solely under diversity and so all venue assessments of claims by plaintiffs must be made pursuant to the terms of §1391(b). With respect to both of the plaintiff's claims, venue would lie under §1391(b)(1) because the defendant resides in the chosen district. Under the definition of corporate residence for venue purposes contained in §1391(c), CBI resides in Lafayette as it clearly is subject to personal jurisdiction there. Plus, venue also would lie under §1391(a)(2) as most of the relevant events occurred in the chosen district. Thus, venue would lie over both claims.

7. Joinder of claims   The plaintiff has asserted two claims against DBI. Under Rule 18, there is no limit to the joinability of claims by one plaintiff against one defendant. So both of these claims are joinable.

II. Emillion v. EIC

1. Choice of law — jurisdictional statute   Since suit was filed in federal court, in the absence of any federal jurisdictional provision, per Rule 4(k)(1), we look to the state jurisdictional statute of the forum state to determine the statutory sufficiency of personal jurisdiction.

2. Statutory basis for personal jurisdiction   EIC insures homes in every state in the country. Thus, it is doing business in every state, including the forum state of Louisiana and so there is a statutory basis for the exercise of personal jurisdiction over EIC. Presumably, EIC is selling policies in the state through its agents and receiving premiums from its policy holders in the forum state.

3. Constitutionality of personal jurisdiction   Having concluded that the long-arm statute applies, we now must determine whether the exercise of that jurisdiction is consistent with the due process requirements of the Fourteenth Amendment. The first portion of this test is the *International Shoe* contacts inquiry. This is a twofold inquiry. First, to what extent, if at all, did the defendant create and maintain a purposeful relationship with the forum state? Second, is the court seeking to exert general or specific jurisdiction?

EIC has agents in the forum state soliciting business and it is receiving premium payments from its insureds in the forum state. It also operates a web page, albeit a relatively passive one that does not permit much, if any, interactivity. But the presence of its agents and the receipt of premiums is certainly enough to create some relationship between the defendant and the forum state. And since the plaintiff's cause of action for failure to honor an insurance contract arises out of those forum activities, the plaintiff is asking the court to exercise specific jurisdiction over the defendant. Under *International Shoe*, the exercise of specific jurisdiction requires a lower threshold of contacts than the exercise of general jurisdiction. EIC's forum contacts justify the exercise of specific jurisdiction.

The second portion of the constitutional test is the application of the "fairness factors" outlined in *Volkswagen*. The plaintiff is a forum citizen and so he has an interest in having the suit heard in Louisiana. The forum state has an interest in providing a forum for the enforcement of contracts entered into by its citizens such as Emillion. The interstate judicial system has an efficiency interest in Louisiana as the forum as some of the witnesses, including the EIC agents, as well as the damaged home, can be found in Louisiana. Therefore, the *Volkswagen* fairness factors further support the exercise of personal jurisdiction over EIC.

4. Subject matter jurisdiction — diversity of citizenship   The plaintiff is a citizen of Louisiana since it is his domicile. The defendant EIC is a citizen of Delaware, its state of incorporation, and Connecticut, the site of its principal place of business. Thus, the parties are diverse. The state law claim is for $250,000, which satisfies the amount in controversy requirement. So this claim falls within the court's diversity jurisdiction under §1332(a).

5. Venue Since there is a federal question asserted by the plaintiff, subject matter jurisdiction over this civil action does not arise solely under diversity and so all venue assessments of claims by plaintiffs must be made pursuant to the terms of §1391(b). With respect to Emillion's claim against EIC, the defendant EIC resides within the chosen district pursuant to the definition of corporate residence for venue purposes found in §1391(c). Thus, venue lies under §1391(b)(1).

6. Joinder of party defendant Plaintiff Emillion seeks to join EIC to his suit that already includes a claim against defendant CBI. Defendants can be joined, pursuant to Rule 20, if there is asserted against all of them claims that (1) arise out of a common series of occurrences or transactions; and (2) contain one single common question of law or fact. Emillion's claims against both defendants arise out of the damage to his home occasioned by the flood. And the question of the extent of the damage to his home is a question common to the claims against both defendants. So they are both joinable.

III. Emillion v. Boudreaux

1. Choice of law — jurisdictional statute Since suit was filed in federal court, in the absence of any federal jurisdictional provision, per Rule 4(k)(1), we look to the state jurisdictional statute of the forum state to determine the statutory sufficiency of personal jurisdiction.

2. Statutory basis for personal jurisdiction As the CEO of CBI, although Boudreaux is now located in California, she undoubtedly has been involved in the business that CBI does in the forum state. So she clearly meets the doing business provision of the Louisiana long-arm statute.

3. Constitutionality of personal jurisdiction Having concluded that the long-arm statute applies, we now must determine whether the exercise of that jurisdiction is consistent with the due process requirements of the Fourteenth Amendment. The first portion of this test is the *International Shoe* contacts inquiry. This is a twofold inquiry. First, to what extent, if at all, did the defendant create and maintain a purposeful relationship with the forum state? Second, is the court seeking to exert general or specific jurisdiction?

Boudreaux previously lived in Louisiana prior to 2005. In addition, her continuing business duties with CBI are centered in Louisiana and so she clearly has a systematic and continuous relationship with the forum state. And since the claim against her arises out of her duties on behalf of CBI in Louisiana, the plaintiff is asking the court to exercise specific jurisdiction over Boudreaux. Under *International Shoe*, the exercise of specific jurisdiction requires a lower threshold of contacts than the exercise of general jurisdiction. Boudreaux's forum contacts justify the exercise of specific jurisdiction.

The second portion of the constitutional test is the application of the "fairness factors" outlined in *Volkswagen*. The plaintiff is a forum citizen and so he has an interest in having the suit heard in Louisiana. The forum state has an interest in providing a forum for the enforcement of contracts entered into by its citizens such as

Emillion. The interstate judicial system has an efficiency interest in Louisiana as the forum as some of the witnesses, including the EIC agents, as well as the damaged home, can be found in Louisiana. Therefore, the *Volkswagen* fairness factors further support the exercise of personal jurisdiction over Boudreaux.

4. Subject matter jurisdiction — diversity of citizenship The plaintiff is a Louisiana citizen as he is domiciled there. Boudreaux is now a California citizen as she has permanently shifted her domicile to Beverly Hills. So the parties are diverse. Emillion asserted a $58,000 claim against Boudreaux, which does not independently meet the amount in controversy requirement of §1332. And under the non-aggregation rules, the plaintiff cannot aggregate the value of this claim with the value of the claims asserted by that plaintiff against other defendants. So there is no original jurisdiction over this claim under §1332.

5. Subject matter jurisdiction — supplemental jurisdiction Can the court exercise supplemental jurisdiction over this state law claim that does not meet §1332's amount in controversy requirement under §1367? In *Exxon Mobil*, the Court said that where a plaintiff's claim against a diverse defendant in a multi-plaintiff case does not meet the amount in controversy requirement, this defect will not contaminate the existence of §1332-based original jurisdiction over other diverse defendants against whom the plaintiff has a state law claim that meets the jurisdictional amount requirement. The Court in *Exxon Mobil* also said that if one of the plaintiffs is not diverse from the defendant, then this destroys complete diversity and, under the contamination theory, does not permit the existence of §1332-based original jurisdiction. And although the plaintiff and defendant CBI are both citizens of Louisiana, since the plaintiff asserted a federal question claim against CBI, the state law claim against CBI fell within the court's supplemental and not diversity-based original jurisdiction. The only other defendant, EIC, is both diverse from the plaintiff and the subject of a claim that meets the amount in controversy requirement. So it would appear that the ruling in *Exxon Mobil* has no application to this civil action.

That leaves for decision the question under §1367 of whether this supplemental claim can be deemed to be part of the same constitutional "case" as a claim within the court's original jurisdiction. It certainly arises out of the same nucleus of operative fact underlying Emillion's federal law claim against Boudreaux's employer, DBI. Thus, it falls within the court's supplemental jurisdiction under §1367(a). And although the trial court has discretion under §1367(c) to dismiss the state law claim, none of the discretionary factors set forth therein would apply here as there is no indication that this state law claim raises novel or complex issues of state law or predominates over the claims by Emillion against CBI. On the other hand, if supplemental jurisdiction over this claim is sought by appending it to the diversity-based claim against EIC, that would raise a different question. There, supplemental jurisdiction would be based on diversity-based original jurisdiction and so the relevant statutory provision would be §1367(b). And that section precludes supplemental jurisdiction over claims by a plaintiff, of which this is one, against a defendant joined under Rule 20. Boudreaux is a party defendant joined under Rule 20 and so the claim against her could not fall within the court's supplemental jurisdiction under §1367(b).

6. Venue   Since there is a federal question claim in this case, venue is assessed for all claims by plaintiff under §1391(b). Venue over the claim against Boudreaux would not lie under §1391(a) because Boudreaux is a resident of California and not of Louisiana. Whether venue would lie under §1391(b)(2) is arguable because the events underlying the claim against Boudreaux could be said to have occurred as much in California as in Louisiana. Venue is not available under §1391(b)(3) as that applies only when no other district is available and venue over this claim clearly could lie in a district in California.

7. Joinder of party defendant   Plaintiff Emillion seeks to join Boudreaux to his suit that already includes a claim against two other defendants. Defendants can be joined, pursuant to Rule 20, if there is asserted against all of them claims that (1) arise out of a common series of occurrences or transactions; and (2) contain one single common question of law or fact. Emillion's claims against both defendants arise out of the repair to his home as a consequence of the flood. And the question of the extent of the damage to his home, as well as the nature of those repairs, is a question common to the claims against both defendants. So Boudreaux is joinable.

IV. CBI v. Boudreaux

1. Personal jurisdiction   The existence of personal jurisdiction over Boudreaux was already discussed in connection with Emillion's claim against Boudreaux. And since this claim is brought by Boudreaux's employer that is located within the forum, the case is even stronger for the exercise of personal jurisdiction.

2. Subject matter jurisdiction — diversity of citizenship   CBI is a citizen of Delaware and Louisiana and Boudreaux is a citizen of California. So the parties are diverse. The indemnity claim is tied to the plaintiff's $250,000 claims so it meets the amount in controversy requirement. The breach of contract claim only involves $35,000 but the cross-plaintiff CBI can aggregate the value of these two claims against Boudreaux to meet the amount in controversy requirement. So original jurisdiction exists over both claims under §1332(a).

3. Joinder of claim   CBI has asserted two cross-claims whose joinability is governed by Rule 13(g), which only permits joinder of a claim that is transactionally related to the original claim or cross-claim. The indemnity claim, by definition, is related to the plaintiff's claim for relief against this cross-plaintiff. But although the breach of contract claim is not transactionally related to the plaintiff's claim and thus not joinable under Rule 13(g), it is joinable as an additional claim under Rule 18.

4. Venue   The requirements of the venue statute only apply to claims by plaintiffs. This is a cross-claim filed by a defendant and so it does not have to be assessed under the venue statute.

V. EIC v. Erich

1. Choice of law — jurisdictional statute   Since suit was filed in federal court, in the absence of any federal jurisdictional provision, per Rule 4(k)(1), we look to the state jurisdictional statute of the forum state to determine the statutory sufficiency of personal jurisdiction.

2. Statutory basis for personal jurisdiction There are no facts suggesting that Erich conducted any of her fraudulent transactions in Louisiana or committed any tortious act in Louisiana that had any consequences in Louisiana. So no statutory basis for jurisdiction over her in Louisiana.

3. Constitutionality of personal jurisdiction Since we concluded that there is no statutory basis for exercising personal jurisdiction, there is no need to discuss this constitutional issue. But, clearly, this defendant has no purposeful contacts with the forum state that would support the exercise of jurisdiction over her in Louisiana.

4. Subject matter jurisdiction — diversity of citizenship The third-party plaintiff, EIC, is a citizen of Delaware and Connecticut. The third-party defendant is a citizen of Connecticut. So the parties are not diverse. The claim is a state law claim so there is no original jurisdiction over this claim.

5. Subject matter jurisdiction — supplemental jurisdiction This claim for fraudulent requests for finder's fees does not arise out of the same operative events of any other claim in the case. Hence, this claim cannot be subject to the exercise of supplemental jurisdiction.

6. Venue Since there is no subject matter jurisdiction over this claim, there is no need to examine venue. Plus, the venue statute would not apply anyway since this is not a claim by a plaintiff.

7. Joinder of claim This is a third-party claim but it is not joinable under Rule 14(a) because it is not a claim for indemnity. So it is not joinable.

QUESTION #2

I. Emillion v. CBI, EIC, and Boudreaux

1. Removal — procedure and subject matter jurisdiction Pursuant to §1441(a), if the case is removable, it will be removed to the district where the state forum is located, i.e., the Western District of Louisiana. The removal statute requires all defendants to join in the removal, which they have done. It also requires the removal to have occurred within 30 days after receipt of the complaint, which they will have to do.

Is the case removable? Emillion's claims against CBI are removable because one is a federal question claim and the other falls within the court's supplemental jurisdiction. Emillion's claim against EIC also is removable because it falls within the court's diversity of citizenship original jurisdiction and EIC is not a citizen of Louisiana, the forum state, so removal is not barred by §1441(b). And the claim against Boudreaux is removable because it also falls within the court's §1367(a) supplemental jurisdiction. So the case is properly removable and will withstand any motion to remand.

2. Transfer Now the question becomes whether the case can be transferred under §1404 to the desired forum — the District of Delaware. The issue here is whether Delaware is a district in which this action might have been brought. That involves a determination of whether all the defendants are subject to personal jurisdiction in Delaware (no consent recognized) and whether venue lies in Delaware over all the claims. Defendants CBI and EIC are citizens of Delaware so no personal jurisdiction problem as to them. But Boudreaux is a California citizen with absolutely no apparent contacts with Delaware so personal jurisdiction could not be exerted over her in Delaware. So the case cannot be transferred there. Moreover, as to venue, while the claims against CBI and EIC would meet the requirements of the venue statute since each of these defendants resides in that district, Boudreaux does not reside there and none of the events involved in the claim against her occurred in Delaware so venue would not lie over the claim against Boudreaux in Delaware. So the case cannot be transferred there.

CIVIL PROCEDURE
MULTIPLE CHOICE
115
QUESTIONS

ANSWER SHEET

Print or copy this answer sheet to all multiple choice questions.

1.	A B C D	30.	A B C D	59.	A B C D	88.	A B C D
2.	A B C D	31.	A B C D	60.	A B C D	89.	A B C D
3.	A B C D	32.	A B C D	61.	A B C D	90.	A B C D
4.	A B C D	33.	A B C D	62.	A B C D	91.	A B C D
5.	A B C D	34.	A B C D	63.	A B C D	92.	A B C D
6.	A B C D	35.	A B C D	64.	A B C D	93.	A B C D
7.	A B C D	36.	A B C D	65.	A B C D	94.	A B C D
8.	A B C D	37.	A B C D	66.	A B C D	95.	A B C D
9.	A B C D	38.	A B C D	67.	A B C D	96.	A B C D
10.	A B C D	39.	A B C D	68.	A B C D	97.	A B C D
11.	A B C D	40.	A B C D	69.	A B C D	98.	A B C D
12.	A B C D	41.	A B C D	70.	A B C D	99.	A B C D
13.	A B C D	42.	A B C D	71.	A B C D	100.	A B C D
14.	A B C D	43.	A B C D	72.	A B C D	101.	A B C D
15.	A B C D	44.	A B C D	73.	A B C D	102.	A B C D
16.	A B C D	45.	A B C D	74.	A B C D	103.	A B C D
17.	A B C D	46.	A B C D	75.	A B C D	104.	A B C D
18.	A B C D	47.	A B C D	76.	A B C D	105.	A B C D
19.	A B C D	48.	A B C D	77.	A B C D	106.	A B C D
20.	A B C D	49.	A B C D	78.	A B C D	107.	A B C D
21.	A B C D	50.	A B C D	79.	A B C D	108.	A B C D
22.	A B C D	51.	A B C D	80.	A B C D	109.	A B C D
23.	A B C D	52.	A B C D	81.	A B C D	110.	A B C D
24.	A B C D	53.	A B C D	82.	A B C D	111.	A B C D
25.	A B C D	54.	A B C D	83.	A B C D	112.	A B C D
26.	A B C D	55.	A B C D	84.	A B C D	113.	A B C D
27.	A B C D	56.	A B C D	85.	A B C D	114.	A B C D
28.	A B C D	57.	A B C D	86.	A B C D	115.	A B C D
29.	A B C D	58.	A B C D	87.	A B C D		

CIVIL PROCEDURE QUESTIONS

Questions 1–5 are based on these facts:

Dan Yankee, a lifelong resident of New York, comes to New Orleans for a Shriner's convention. One night while imbibing in the Devil's Brew, he tasted a local whiskey, Raging Cajun. Liking what he tasted, he bought a case of Raging Cajun to take back to New York. Upon his return to New York, Dan gave a bottle of Raging Cajun to his boss, Ben Bunkley, a citizen of New York. After work that evening, Bunkley decided to try the Raging Cajun and prepared himself a cocktail consisting of Raging Cajun and water. After three or four sips of his cocktail, Bunkley experienced a severe burning sensation in his throat and stomach. He called his doctor, who advised him to come to the hospital and bring the bottle of Raging Cajun with him. At the hospital it was determined that the bottle of Raging Cajun contained a high percentage of acid. Bunkley was treated accordingly. He survived, but had to have part of his stomach removed and will talk in a low raspy voice for the rest of his life. Bunkley's doctor and hospital bills were in excess of $25,000.

Bunkley comes to you, an attorney in New York, and wants you to represent him in his personal injury action. He wants to sue for $1 million to pay for his medical expenses and be compensated for his pain and suffering and permanent physical impairments. You agree to represent him and immediately begin making certain investigations. You learn that Raging Cajun is a product distilled by the Acadia Whiskey Company, a Louisiana corporation with its principal place of business in Louisiana. It distributes its products in Louisiana, Alabama, and Mississippi. You learn that about 45% of all sales of Raging Cajun are made to New York tourists who take the product back to their home state and 50% of its sales are made to New Yorkers who purchase the liquor through Acadia's highly interactive web site. Sales to New Yorkers account for in excess of $3 million annually. In addition, you learn that Acadia Whiskey Company has $500,000 on deposit in a New York bank.

Assume that the legislature in every state in the country has passed the following statute:

> The courts of this state shall have personal jurisdiction over an individual, corporation or other entity who, in person or through an agent:
> (1) transacts business within the state; or
> (2) commits a tortious act without the state causing injury within the state; or
> (3) is personally served within the state; or
> (4) owns property within the state.

1. Can a state court in New York exercise specific jurisdiction over Acadia Whiskey Company?

    A) Yes, because Acadia transacts business in New York and the cause of action arose out of those contacts.

    B) Yes, because of the presence of Acadia's bank account in New York.

C) No, because it did not commit a tortious act in New York.

D) No, because Acadia has no contacts with New York.

2. Can a state court in Louisiana exercise specific jurisdiction over Acadia Whiskey Company?

   A) No, because it does not have a bank account in Louisiana.

   B) Yes, because it transacts business in Louisiana.

   C) No, because it did not commit a tortious act in Louisiana.

   D) Yes, because it is a citizen of Louisiana.

3. Can a state court in New York exercise *quasi in rem* jurisdiction over Acadia?

   A) Yes, because Acadia is transacting business in New York.

   B) Yes, because Acadia committed a tortious act in New York.

   C) Yes, because Acadia has a bank account in New York.

   D) Yes, because Acadia has a bank account in New York and because it has other contacts with the forum state.

4. Can the state courts in Alabama and Mississippi exercise general jurisdiction over Acadia?

   A) No, because Acadia does not have a bank account there.

   B) Yes, because Acadia does some business there.

   C) No, because Acadia did not commit a tortious act there.

   D) No, because Acadia does not have sufficient contacts there.

5. If the plaintiff chose to file this action in a federal district court in New York, which long-arm statute would apply?

   A) Louisiana because the defendant is a citizen of that state.

   B) New York because the plaintiff is a citizen of that state.

   C) Louisiana because that is where the tortious act occurred.

   D) New York because it is the forum state.

6. John Henry, a lifetime resident of Boston, made his first ever foray out of Massachusetts when he flew to Los Angeles. He was unable to get a nonstop flight and so had to change planes at John F. Kennedy International Airport in New York City. While sitting in a coffee shop at the airport, he was served with process in connection with a lawsuit filed against him by his former next-door neighbor. His neighbor, now a citizen of New York, brought suit in New York claiming that

John had sold him a lemon — John's 2007 automobile. Can the New York court exercise personal jurisdiction over John?

A) No, because the car sale was consummated in Massachusetts.

B) Yes, because the plaintiff is a citizen of New York.

C) No, because John is a citizen of Massachusetts.

D) Yes, because John was served in New York.

Questions 7 and 8 are based on these facts:

Plaintiff files a claim against the defendant, a Delaware corporation with its headquarters located in New York, in federal district court in Los Angeles alleging a violation of the federal antitrust statute, which contains a provision for nationwide service of process. The defendant is a major retailer with retail shops in all 50 states and a highly interactive web page that generates hundreds of thousands of dollars of business annually from citizens of all 50 states.

7. Which jurisdictional statute governs whether or not the defendant is subject to personal jurisdiction?

A) California law because California is the forum state.

B) Delaware law because the defendant is a Delaware citizen.

C) New York law because the defendant's headquarters are there.

D) The federal antitrust statute.

8. The determination of whether the exercise of personal jurisdiction over the defendant meets constitutional standards will depend upon an analysis of:

A) Whether the defendant's contacts with the forum state meet the due process requirements of the Fourteenth Amendment.

B) Whether the defendant's contacts with the forum state meet the due process requirements of the Fifth Amendment.

C) Whether the defendant's contacts within the United States as a whole meet the due process requirements of the Fifth Amendment.

D) There is no need to evaluate the constitutionality of the exercise of personal jurisdiction in this context.

9. The plaintiff, a Connecticut citizen, brings an action against the defendant, an Ohio corporation, in federal district court in Connecticut asserting two claims. The first claim alleges a violation of the federal antitrust law, which provides for nationwide service of process. The second claim is for breach of contract with respect to an underlined matter. The trial court has determined that it can constitutionally exercise personal jurisdiction over the defendant with respect to the federal claim. It has also determined that the defendant is not subject to personal jurisdiction under the terms of the Connecticut long-arm statute. Can the court exercise personal jurisdiction over the defendant with respect to the entire case?

A) No, because there is no personal jurisdiction under the Connecticut long-arm statute.

B) Yes, because of the doctrine of pendent personal jurisdiction.

C) Yes, because federal law trumps state law under the Supremacy Clause of the U.S. Constitution.

D) No, because the federal and state law claims do not arise out of a common nucleus of operative fact.

10. In a tort action filed in a federal district court in Alabama by an Alabama plaintiff against a citizen of California, the defendant refuses to waive service of process. The accident that gave rise to the lawsuit occurred in Mississippi. The plaintiff wants to serve the defendant while the defendant is on vacation in New York City. Which statute governs the sufficiency of service in this case?

A) California law because the defendant is a citizen of that state.

B) Federal statute because suit was brought in a federal court.

C) New York law because the defendant is being served there.

D) Mississippi law because the accident occurred in Mississippi.

11. In an action filed in federal district court, the defendant refuses to waive service. So the plaintiff serves the defendant by placing a copy of the summons and complaint in the hands of the defendant's housekeeper while she is working in the defendant's home. She forgets to turn it over to the defendant. Is this service proper under the Federal Rules of Civil Procedure?

A) Yes, because the housekeeper is in the defendant's home.

B) No, because the defendant was not personally served.

C) Yes, because the housekeeper is a person of suitable age and discretion.

D) No, because the housekeeper does not reside in the defendant's home.

12. In an action filed in federal district court, the defendant refuses to waive service. The defendant owns homes in New York, California, and Florida, spending time in each place at different times of the year. The plaintiff serves the defendant's wife at the Florida home while the defendant is staying at the California home. She forgets to transfer the process to the defendant. Is this service proper under the Federal Rules of Civil Procedure?

A) No, because the defendant was in California.

B) Yes, because the Florida home is the defendant's dwelling house or usual place of abode.

C) No, because the defendant did not receive the process.

D) Yes, because the recipient is his wife.

13. In a breach of contract action filed in federal district court by a Nevada plaintiff against a Virginia defendant, the defendant refuses to waive service. The plaintiff serves the woman, who had represented the defendant in his previous divorce, at her law office. Is this service proper under the Federal Rules of Civil Procedure?

A) Yes, because she is the defendant's attorney.

B) No, because she was not authorized to receive service.

C) No, because she was served at her office and not at the defendant's home.

D) No, because she does not live in the defendant's home.

14. The plaintiff, a Vermont citizen, bought a television from the defendant retailer, an Illinois corporation. The written sales agreement provides that the purchaser designated the company president's secretary to receive service of process for the customer in any action brought by the retailer under the terms of this agreement. When the customer failed to make a payment, the retailer sued him for breach of contract in federal district court and served the company president's secretary. The secretary, who was unknown to the defendant, mails a copy of the service to the defendant's home and the defendant receives it. Is this service proper under the Federal Rules of Civil Procedure?

A) Yes, because the defendant agreed to it by signing the contract, and received the process.

B) No, because this is a form contract and the service provision was in small type.

C) No, because the secretary was unknown to the defendant and was the plaintiff's employee.

D) Yes, because the secretary was paid for being a recipient of service.

15. The plaintiff and defendant assert ownership to the same home located in California. The plaintiff is a California citizen and the defendant, the plaintiff's former best friend, is a citizen of West Virginia. The plaintiff files suit in federal court in California and the defendant refuses to waive service. The plaintiff obtains a court order seizing the property and serves the defendant by publication in a Los Angeles publication. The defendant, who stopped corresponding with the defendant one week before suit was brought, files a

motion to dismiss for insufficient service. Should the court grant the defense motion?

A) No, because the property was seized.

B) No, because service was effected by publication.

C) Yes, because the plaintiff knew the defendant's location and could have mailed service to the defendant's home address.

D) Yes, because this is an *in personam* proceeding.

16. The plaintiff, a New York citizen, brings an action in federal district court alleging that the defendant, also a New York citizen, agreed to purchase his home and subsequently refused to go forward with the deal. The defendant's answer admits that he refused to buy the home but alleges that because the plaintiff had lied in certain representations about the home contained in a federally required disclosure form, the deal was unenforceable under the governing federal disclosure statute. Does the court have subject matter jurisdiction?

A) Yes, because this case arises under federal law.

B) No, because this case does not arise under federal law.

C) Yes, because the defendant filed an answer, waiving his jurisdictional objection.

D) No, because the parties are citizens of the same state.

17. The plaintiff, a New York citizen, brings an action in federal district court alleging that the defendant, also a New York citizen, agreed to purchase his home and subsequently refused to go forward with the deal. In his complaint, the plaintiff alleges that even if he misrepresented important features of the home in violation of the requirements of federal disclosure law, this statute is unconstitutional. Does the court have subject matter jurisdiction?

A) Yes, because this case arises under federal law.

B) No, because this case does not arise under federal law and the parties are citizens of the same state.

C) Yes, because the defendant filed an answer, waiving his jurisdictional objection.

D) No, because the parties are citizens of the same state.

18. The plaintiff, a Vermont citizen, files a claim in federal district court alleging that the defendant, a Delaware corporation, violated his rights under the federal Civil Rights Act of 1964 and seeks damages in the amount of $50,000. Does the court have subject matter jurisdiction?

A) No, because the plaintiff is seeking only $50,000.

B) No, because the claim does not arise under federal law.

C) Yes, because the parties are diverse.

D) Yes, because the claim arises under federal law.

19. The plaintiff, a Vermont citizen, files a claim in state court alleging that the defendant, a Delaware corporation, violated his rights under the federal Civil Rights Act of 1964 and seeks damages in the amount of $50,000. Does the state court have subject matter jurisdiction?

A) Yes, because the parties are diverse.

B) Yes, because the Civil Rights Act does not provide for exclusive federal court jurisdiction.

C) Yes, because this claim arises under federal law.

D) No, because the plaintiff is seeking only $50,000.

20. The plaintiff believes that she has been discriminated against on the basis of her sex in violation of both federal and state law. But she wants to avoid being in federal court and so she files a complaint in state court asserting only a claim under the state antidiscrimination statute. Assuming the parties are not of diverse citizenship, will she be successful in staying out of federal court?

A) No, because she could state a claim arising under federal law.

B) Yes, because of the "master of the complaint" doctrine.

C) No, because of the "artful pleading" doctrine.

D) Yes, because the parties are not diverse.

21. An Illinois plaintiff files a breach of contract claim in federal court against a defendant who had been born and raised in North Dakota. The defendant moved to Chicago to attend college and law school in the hope of practicing law in his home town. The plaintiff's claim is for $100,000. Does the court have subject matter jurisdiction?

A) Yes, because the parties are diverse and because the claim is in excess of $75,000.

B) No, because the parties are not diverse.

C) No, because both parties reside in Illinois.

D) Yes, because the claim is in excess of $75,000.

Questions 22–24 are based on these facts:

Sheila Webb, a Utah citizen, purchased educational software programs invented by Simon Quant and sold by Early Bird, Inc. Simon has dual nationality;

he is a citizen of both the United States and Germany. He permanently resides in Santa Fe, New Mexico. Early Bird is incorporated under the laws of Delaware and has its headquarters and warehouse located in Provo, Utah. Early Bird also has retail outlets in Chicago, New York, and Los Angeles. Sheila's aunt, Margaret Welch, who also bought some of the same software, is a citizen of Germany.

22. Sheila files a breach of contract action against Early Bird in federal court in Provo. She seeks $150,000 in damages. Does the court have subject matter jurisdiction?

A) Yes, because the parties are diverse.

B) No, because the parties are not diverse.

C) Yes, because the defendant is not a citizen of the forum state.

D) No, because Early Bird has no contacts with Utah.

23. Sheila files a lawsuit asserting one breach of contract claim against Simon and one breach of contract claim against Early Bird in federal court in Provo. She seeks $150,000 in damages in connection with each claim. Does the court have subject matter jurisdiction?

A) Yes, because Simon is a citizen of New Mexico.

B) No, because Early Bird is a citizen of Utah.

C) Yes, because each claim is for $150,000.

D) No, because the suit should have been filed in Delaware.

24. Sheila and Margaret joined in an action against both Simon and Early Bird. The suit was filed in federal court in Utah. All the claims are for breach of contract and each plaintiff sought $100,000 in connection with each claim. Does the court have subject matter jurisdiction?

A) No, because aliens cannot file a claim in federal court.

B) No, because Margaret and Simon are both citizens of Germany.

C) No, because Early Bird is a citizen of Utah.

D) Yes, because each claim is for $100,000.

25. A Texas plaintiff brought a tort action in federal court in Texas against a defendant who was a citizen of both Italy and the United States and who was permanently domiciled in Texas. The claim is for $100,000. Does the court have subject matter jurisdiction?

A) Yes, because the defendant is an alien.

B) No, because the defendant is a citizen of Texas.

C) No, because aliens cannot be sued in federal court.

D) Yes, because the claim is for $100,000.

26. A Virginia plaintiff brought a breach of contract claim in federal court in Virginia against a dual national who was a citizen of both the United States and France. The defendant had left the United States ten years earlier and set up permanent residence in Paris, where he intends to remain for the rest of his life. The claim is for $100,000. Does the federal court have subject matter jurisdiction?

A) Yes, because the defendant is a French citizen.

B) No, because the defendant is domiciled in Paris.

C) Yes, because the claim is for $100,000.

D) No, because the defendant has no contacts with Virginia.

27. A citizen of Pennsylvania is injured in a car accident with another citizen of that same state who was not injured in the crash. The injured party is in desperate need of cash and so he assigns his cause of action to a citizen of New York for $50,000. The New Yorker then files the claim in federal court in New York, seeking damages in the amount of $100,000. Does the court have subject matter jurisdiction?

A) No, because the parties are not diverse.

B) Yes, because the parties are diverse and the claim is for $100,000.

C) No, because this is a collusive assignment.

D) Yes, because the citizen is a citizen of New York.

28. A citizen of Pennsylvania is injured in a car accident with another citizen of that same state who was not injured in the crash. The injured party assigned his claim to a New York citizen on the understanding that the New Yorker would transfer all proceeds recovered at trial back to the injured party in exchange for a fee for expenses and services provided. The New Yorker then files the claim in federal court in Pennsylvania, seeking damages in the amount of $100,000. Does the court have subject matter jurisdiction?

A) Yes, because all §1332(a)(1) requirements are met.

B) No, because the parties are not diverse.

C) Yes, because this is not a collusive assignment.

D) No, because the defendant is a citizen of Pennsylvania.

29. A citizen of Oregon was injured in an accident by a citizen of Wyoming. Before filing suit in state court, the Oregonian assigned his claim to a citizen

of Wyoming on the understanding that the Wyoming citizen would transfer all proceeds recovered at trial back to the injured party in exchange for a fee for expenses and services provided. This individual then filed the suit seeking $100,000 in damages in Oregon state court. The defendant sought to remove the case on the basis of diversity jurisdiction. Does the federal court have subject matter jurisdiction?

A) Yes, because the parties are diverse and the claim is for $100,000.

B) No, because the claim arises under state law.

C) No, because the parties are not diverse.

D) Yes, because §1359 is inapplicable.

30. A Louisiana citizen brings a tort claim against two Texas citizens in a federal court in Texas. The claim against each defendant is for $250,000. Does the court have subject matter jurisdiction?

A) No, because the defendants are both citizens of the same state.

B) No, because the defendants are citizens of the forum state.

C) Yes, because the adverse parties are of diverse citizenship.

D) No, because the claim does not arise under federal law.

31. A citizen of the State of Washington brought a $230,000 tort claim in federal court against a citizen of Spain. The defendant was lawfully admitted to reside permanently in the United States and had decided to live in the State of Washington for the remainder of his life. Does the court have subject matter jurisdiction?

A) Yes, because the defendant is an alien.

B) No, because the parties are not diverse.

C) Yes, because the claim is for $230,000.

D) No, because aliens cannot be sued in federal court.

32. A Nevada plaintiff brings a tort claim in federal court in Ohio for $35,000 and a separate breach of contract claim for $55,000 against a single Ohio defendant. Does the court have subject matter jurisdiction?

A) Yes, because the parties are of diverse citizenship.

B) No, because the defendant is a citizen of the forum state.

C) Yes, because the complaint seeks $90,000 in damages and the parties are diverse.

D) No, because the complaint does not satisfy the jurisdictional amount in controversy requirement.

33. A victim of an automobile accident brings claims against both the owner and the driver of the car that caused the accident in one lawsuit. All three participants are citizens of different states. The plaintiff seeks $40,000 in damages against each of the defendants. Does the court have subject matter jurisdiction?

A) Yes, because the parties are citizens of different states.

B) No, because the complaint does not satisfy the jurisdictional amount in controversy requirement.

C) Yes, because the complaint seeks $80,000 in damages and the parties are diverse.

D) No, because the claim does not arise under federal law.

34. A victim of an automobile accident brings claims against both the owner and the driver of the car that caused the accident in one lawsuit. All three participants are citizens of different states. The plaintiff seeks $75,000 damages against each of the defendants. Does the court have subject matter jurisdiction?

A) Yes, because the parties are citizens of different states.

B) No, because the complaint does not satisfy the jurisdictional amount in controversy requirement.

C) Yes, because the complaint does satisfy the jurisdictional amount in controversy requirement.

D) No, because the claim does not arise under federal law.

35. Two Texas citizens join in one civil action to bring separate breach of contract claims against a citizen of Alabama. Each plaintiff's claim seeks $50,000 in damages against the defendant. The suit is brought in federal court in Alabama. Does the court have subject matter jurisdiction?

A) Yes, because the adverse parties are of diverse citizenship.

B) No, because the defendants are citizens of the forum state.

C) Yes, because the claims against the defendant are in excess of $75,000 and the parties are of diverse citizenship.

D) No, because the complaint does not satisfy the jurisdictional amount in controversy requirement.

36. A New Hampshire plaintiff brings an $85,000 tort claim against a Delaware defendant in federal court in Delaware. After trial, the jury awards the plaintiff $70,000. Can the defendant successfully move to dismiss the case for lack of subject matter jurisdiction?

A) No, because by going to trial the defendant has waived his objection to any defect in subject matter jurisdiction.

B) Yes, because the case did not meet the jurisdictional amount in controversy requirement.

C) No, because the claim meets all requirements of §1332(a)(1).

D) Yes, because the defendant is a citizen of the forum state.

37. The plaintiff, a citizen of New Mexico, brought a tort claim for medical malpractice in federal court in Utah against her Utah-based physician alleging that an operation performed on January 1, 2007 was botched. Her complaint sought $1 million in damages. The jury rendered a verdict in favor of the defendant physician, finding her non-negligent. One year later, the plaintiff filed another malpractice claim in federal court against the same doctor, alleging that the botched operation has caused additional, minor injuries to her that manifested only after the completion of the first trial. In this action, the plaintiff seeks $1 million for her prior injuries and $50,000 for the additional injuries. Does the court have subject matter jurisdiction?

A) Yes, because the defendant is a citizen of Utah.

B) No, because the plaintiff has already recovered $1 million and so the real amount in controversy does not exceed $75,000.

C) Yes, because all requirements of §1332(a)(1) have been met.

D) No, because the action is barred by claim preclusion.

38. As required by the arbitration clause contained in his employment agreement, a discharged employee was compelled to bring his claim of disability-based discrimination to an arbitrator. After the arbitrator ruled in favor of the employer and awarded $50,000, the employee filed an action in federal district court to vacate the arbitration award on the ground that the arbitration agreement constituted an unenforceable contract of adhesion. Although the case does not present a federal question, the parties are diverse. The employee's claim before the arbitrator included a request for $150,000 in lost wages. Does the court have subject matter jurisdiction?

A) Yes, because the claim before the arbitrator was for $150,000.

B) No, because the arbitrator awarded only $50,000.

C) Yes, because the parties are of diverse citizenship.

D) No, because the case does not present a federal question.

39. A young child's grandfather, a Colorado citizen, brought an action in federal court in Maine against his own son, a citizen of Honduras, seeking custody of the plaintiff's grandson. Does the court have subject matter jurisdiction?

A) No, because the complaint does not seek any monetary damages, the amount in controversy requirement has not been met.

B) Yes, under §1332(a)(2) alienage jurisdiction.

C) No, because the federal courts cannot hear domestic relations cases such as this.

D) Yes, if the value of the right asserted by the plaintiff is assessed to be in excess of $75,000.

40. A divorced mother domiciled in Idaho filed an action in federal court in New Jersey against her former husband, a citizen of New Jersey, for $250,000 in damages alleging that he had abused her and her children. Does the court have subject matter jurisdiction?

A) Yes, because the requirements of §1332(a)(1) have been met.

B) No, because federal courts cannot hear domestic relations cases such as this.

C) Yes, because the action was brought in the defendant's home.

D) No, because the defendant is a citizen of the forum state.

41. A citizen of Indiana brings an action against her employer, an Indiana corporation, in federal district court. Claim one alleges that she was discriminated against on the basis of her sex in violation of the federal Civil Rights Act of 1964. The second claim consists of a tort claim for intentional infliction of emotional distress arising out of the same series of acts of sexual harassment that formed the basis of her federal sex discrimination claim. The plaintiff seeks $250,000 in damages in connection with each claim. Does the court have subject matter jurisdiction over the entire lawsuit?

A) Not over the second claim because it is a nondiverse state law claim.

B) Yes, because the two claims arise out of a common nucleus of operative fact and there is no reason to decline to exercise supplemental jurisdiction over the state claim.

C) No, because the defendant is a citizen of the forum state.

D) Yes, because federal courts have concurrent jurisdiction over most federal law claims.

42. A citizen of Indiana brings an action against her employer, an Indiana corporation, in federal district court. Claim one alleges that she was discriminated against on the basis of her sex in violation of the federal Civil Rights Act of 1964. The second claim consists of a tort claim for negligent infliction of emotional distress arising out of the same series of acts of sexual harassment that formed the basis of her federal sex discrimination claim. The plaintiff seeks $100,000 in compensatory damages and $1 million in punitive damages under each of these two claims. The availability of punitive damages in negligent infliction of emotional distress cases has not previously been addressed under the governing Indiana state law. Should the court exercise subject matter jurisdiction over the entire lawsuit?

A) Yes, because the two claims arise out of a common nucleus of operative fact.

B) Not over the state law claim because the parties are not diverse.

C) Yes, because the issues raised in the two claims are nearly identical.

D) Not over the state law claim because it raises a novel issue of state law.

43. A purchaser of a television brought an action against the manufacturer in federal district court in Massachusetts containing a claim that the manufacturer participated in a conspiracy to engage in unlawful price-fixing in violation of the federal antitrust laws. The plaintiff is a citizen of Massachusetts and the defendant is a citizen of Delaware and Massachusetts. In his complaint, the plaintiff also asserted a breach of contract claim, alleging that the television was defective and that the manufacturer refused to honor the warranty contained in the purchase agreement. In connection with this second claim, the plaintiff seeks $100,000 in damages. Can the court exercise subject matter jurisdiction over the entire lawsuit?

A) No, because both parties are citizens of Massachusetts.

B) Yes, because the court can exercise supplemental jurisdiction over the state claim and §1331 jurisdiction over the federal claim.

C) No, because the claims do not arise out of a common nucleus of operative fact.

D) Yes, because the value of the state claim exceeds $75,000.

44. A Wyoming plaintiff files an action in federal court in South Dakota against a South Dakota citizen. The complaint consists of a $100,000 tort claim and a completely unrelated $50,000 breach of contract action. Can the court exercise subject matter jurisdiction over the entire case?

A) Yes, under §1367.

B) No, because the two claims do not form part of the same case.

C) Yes, under §1332.

D) No, because the defendant is a citizen of the forum state.

45. A Nevada citizen brought a patent infringement claim against Acme Products, a Delaware corporation, in federal court in Nevada. The plaintiff alleged that Acme had infringed his patent in violation of the federal patent statute and sought damages in the amount of $65,000. The plaintiff also asserted a $250,000 intentional infliction of emotional distress claim against the president of Acme, Roy Jones, a citizen of Nevada. In this claim, the plaintiff alleges that Jones, acting on behalf of Acme, engaged in the infringing conduct and that this caused the plaintiff to suffer severe emotional distress. Can the court exercise subject matter jurisdiction over the entire lawsuit?

A) Yes, under §1367(a).

B) No, because courts do not permit pendent party jurisdiction.

C) Yes, because the value of the two claims can be aggregated.

D) No, because he sought less than $75,000 in his patent infringement claim.

46. A Nevada citizen brought a patent infringement claim against Acme Products, a Delaware corporation, in federal court in Nevada. The plaintiff alleged that Acme had infringed his patent in violation of the federal patent statute and sought damages in the amount of $65,000. The plaintiff also asserted a $250,000 intentional infliction of emotional distress claim against the president of Acme, Roy Jones, a citizen of Nevada. In this claim, the plaintiff alleges that Jones had subjected her to a repeated series of acts of sexual harassment and that this caused the plaintiff to suffer severe emotional distress. Can the court exercise subject matter jurisdiction over the entire lawsuit?

A) Yes, under §1367(a).

B) No, because courts do not permit pendent party jurisdiction.

C) Yes, because the value of the two claims can be aggregated.

D) No, because the two claims do not form part of the same case.

47. Vernon, a Louisiana citizen, was riding in a car driven by his friend Paul, a Texas citizen. They crashed into a car driven by Luther, a Texas citizen. Vernon and Paul filed an action in federal court in Texas in which each of the plaintiffs asserted a $150,000 tort action against Paul. Does the court have subject matter jurisdiction over the entire lawsuit?

A) Yes, under §1332 and §1367(a).

B) No, because Paul and Luther are both Texas citizens.

C) Yes, because each claim is for more than $75,000.

D) No, because the action was filed in Texas.

Questions 48–52 are based on these facts:

Randolph Paine, a citizen of New York, and his sister, Jane Summers, a New York citizen, filed an action in federal court in Delaware against Summit, Inc., a Delaware corporation with a New York principal place of business, alleging that the prospectus issued by Summit in connection with the sale of its stock contained misrepresentations in violation of both federal securities law and Delaware corporate law. In connection with that claim, Randolph and Paine each sought $350,000 in damages. Paine and Summers also, in that same lawsuit, asserted a $350,000 claim against Holcomb Brothers, a stock brokerage partnership, all of whose partners are citizens of New York, alleging that Holcomb had distributed these prospectuses in full knowledge of the existence of these material representations in violation of Delaware law. Holcomb in turn filed a $400,000 breach of contract claim against Summit alleging that Summit failed to pay its commission earned by selling shares of Summit. Summit filed a $2 million claim against the plaintiffs under state law for malicious prosecution and a claim against Leroy Williams, a citizen of New York and the author of the prospectus, seeking indemnification from any recovery Paine and Summers might obtain from it under their federal claim.

48. Does the court have subject matter jurisdiction over Paine and Summers' claims against Summit?

A) Yes, over both under §1331.

B) Not over the state corporate law claim because it does not arise under federal law.

C) Yes, under §1331 and §1367.

D) Not over the plaintiffs' state law claims because the parties are not diverse.

49. Does the court have subject matter jurisdiction over Paine and Summers' claims against Holcomb Brothers?

A) Yes, under §1367.

B) No, because the adverse parties are not diverse.

C) Yes, because the claims seek damages in excess of $75,000.

D) No, because suit was filed in Delaware.

50. Does the court have subject matter jurisdiction over Holcomb's claim against Summit?

A) Yes, because the claim is in excess of $75,000.

B) No, because the parties are not diverse.

C) Yes, because it falls within the court's supplemental jurisdiction.

D) No, because the claim is unrelated to the plaintiffs' claims against Summit.

51. Does the court have subject matter jurisdiction over Summit's indemnity claim against Williams?

A) No, because it is a nondiverse state law claim.

B) Yes, because it falls within the court's supplemental jurisdiction.

C) No, because it is unrelated to the plaintiffs' claims against Summit.

D) Yes, because it seeks damages in excess of $75,000.

52. Does the court have subject matter jurisdiction over Summit's claim against the plaintiffs?

A) No, because the parties are not diverse.

B) Yes, because it seeks damages in excess of $75,000.

C) No, because it is unrelated to the plaintiff's claims against Summit.

D) Yes, because it falls within the court's supplemental jurisdiction.

Questions 53–56 are based on these facts:

A Rhode Island plaintiff brings a $250,000 tort claim in federal court in Missouri against a Missouri defendant and a $170,000 tort claim against a Rhode Island defendant. The Rhode Island defendant responds by filing an unrelated $60,000 breach of contract claim against the plaintiff and the plaintiff's father, a citizen of Missouri. The Rhode Island defendant files an unrelated $50,000 breach of contract claim against the Missouri defendant.

53. Does the court have subject matter jurisdiction over the plaintiff's claim against the Rhode Island defendant?

A) No, because the presence of that defendant destroys complete diversity.

B) No, because the claim is unrelated to the plaintiff's claim against the other defendant.

C) Yes, because the claim falls within the court's supplemental jurisdiction.

D) Yes, because the claim is for $170,000.

54. Does the court have subject matter jurisdiction over the Rhode Island defendant's claim against the plaintiff?

A) Yes, because it falls under §1367(a) supplemental jurisdiction.

B) No, because there is no claim falling within the court's original jurisdiction.

C) Yes, because the defendant is a citizen of the forum state.

D) No, because this claim is unrelated to the plaintiff's claim against the other defendant.

55. Does the court have subject matter jurisdiction over the Rhode Island defendant's claim against the plaintiff's father?

A) Yes, because the adverse parties to this claim are diverse.

B) Yes, under §1367(a).

C) No, because there is no claim falling within the court's original jurisdiction.

D) No, because this claim is unrelated to the plaintiff's claim against the other defendant.

56. Does the court have subject matter jurisdiction over the Rhode Island defendant's claim against the Missouri defendant?

A) Yes, because the parties are diverse.

B) No, because of §1367(b).

C) Yes, because of §1367(a).

D) No, because there is no claim falling within the court's original jurisdiction.

57. Ace Construction, Inc., a citizen of Delaware and West Virginia, brought an action in federal court in Pennsylvania against the Construction Workers Union Local #25, all but two of whose members were domiciled in Pennsylvania. The union's other two members were domiciled in nearby West Virginia. The company sought $150,000 in damages. A few days before trial, both members from West Virginia quit the union. After the jury rendered a verdict in favor of the plaintiff, but before the trial court entered judgment on the verdict, the defendant moved to dismiss the case on the ground of lack of subject matter jurisdiction. How should the court rule on the motion?

A) Deny it because the defendant waived the objection by going to trial on the merits.

B) Grant it because the parties were not diverse.

C) Deny it because the parties were diverse once the West Virginians left the union.

D) Grant it because the defendant is a citizen of the forum state.

58. Brice Construction, Inc., a South Dakota corporation filed a $250,000 breach of contract action in federal court in North Dakota asserting claims against Apples, Inc., a North Dakota corporation and Oranges, Inc., a South Dakota corporation. About a month before trial, Oranges, Inc. was dismissed from the case. The case went to trial and the jury rendered a verdict in favor of the plaintiff. Before the trial judge entered judgment on the verdict, the defendant moved to dismiss the case for lack of subject matter jurisdiction. How should the court rule on the motion?

A) Deny it because the defendant waived the objection by going to trial.

B) Grant it because the parties were not diverse when the complaint was filed.

C) Deny it because the dismissal of Oranges, Inc. cured the defect in diversity.

D) Grant it because the remaining defendant was a citizen of the forum state.

59. A Virginia plaintiff filed an action against a Virginia defendant in federal court in Virginia. The complaint contained a claim alleging a violation of a federal environmental statute and a totally unrelated tort claim. The plaintiff sought $300,000 in connection with each claim. In response to a defense motion, the trial court dismissed the state law claim for lack of subject matter jurisdiction. Two months later, the plaintiff then filed that state claim in a Virginia state court. But by that time, the limitations period set forth by the governing statute of limitations had expired. How should the state court rule on the defendant's motion to dismiss the suit on the ground that the claim had expired?

A) Deny it because the state claim had been filed in federal court before the expiration of the limitations period.

B) Grant it because the plaintiff waited two months to refile in state court.

C) Deny it because the state limitations period is tolled.

D) Grant it because the federal court complaint contained a federal statutory claim.

60. Herbert Kraft, a Massachusetts citizen, brought a federal civil rights claim against Lisa Hall, a Massachusetts citizen, and a state law claim against the State of Massachusetts in a suit filed in federal court in Massachusetts. The trial court dismissed the claim against the state on the ground that the state enjoyed sovereign immunity against such a claim under the Eleventh Amendment to the U.S. Constitution. One week after that ruling, Mr. Kraft refiled that claim in a Massachusetts state court. But by that time, the limitations period contained in the relevant state statute of limitations had expired. Should the state court dismiss the case on the ground that the claim had expired?

A) Yes, because the claim had expired under state law.

B) No, because the plaintiff refiled less than 30 days after the claim was dismissed.

C) Yes, because this was a claim against a state.

D) No, because claims against states are not subject to limitation periods.

61. An Arizona citizen filed an action in New Mexico state court against the police department of Scottsdale, Arizona. In her complaint, the plaintiff alleged that she had been a victim of sexual harassment as the result of a barrage of sexual insults directed at her by several of her supervisors. On the basis of these factual allegations, she asserted a tort claim for intentional infliction of emotional distress for which she sought damages in the amount of $1 million. In her complaint the plaintiff also alleged that the sexual remarks were not protected by the First and Fourteenth Amendments just because they were made by government workers. Is this action properly removable?

A) Yes, because the federal court had original jurisdiction over the plaintiff's claim.

B) No, because state agencies cannot remove cases.

C) Yes, because the claim is in excess of $75,000.

D) No, because the federal court did not have original jurisdiction over the plaintiff's claim.

62. An Arizona citizen filed an action in New Mexico state court against the police department of Scottsdale, Arizona. In her complaint, the plaintiff alleged that she had been a victim of sexual harassment as the result of a barrage of sexual insults directed at her by several of her supervisors. On the basis of these factual allegations, she asserted a tort claim for intentional infliction of emotional distress for which she sought damages in the amount of $50,000. The defendant seeks to remove the case on the ground that since sexual harassment is prohibited under the federal Civil Rights Act of 1964, the plaintiff's failure to assert this claim cannot deprive the federal court of its original jurisdiction over a federal statutory claim. Is the case properly removable?

A) No, because the parties are not citizens of different states.

B) Yes, because the plaintiff could and should have asserted a federal statutory claim.

C) No, because the plaintiff did not assert a statutory claim and federal law does not preempt the field.

D) Yes, because the defendant is a citizen of the forum state.

63. A California citizen living on the border with Arizona filed an action in California state court against an Arizona citizen seeking an injunction to stop the construction of a weather tower on the defendant's property. The plaintiff argued that the injunction was proper because the construction of the tower would constitute a nuisance under state tort law. The complaint also asserts an unrelated breach of contract claim seeking $75,000 in damages. Is the case properly removable?

A) No, because the claim does not exceed $75,000.

B) Yes, because the federal court has original jurisdiction under §1331.

C) No, because the defendant is a citizen of the forum state.

D) Yes, because the federal court has original jurisdiction under §1332.

64. A California citizen living on the border with Arizona filed an action in Arizona state court against an Arizona citizen alleging that the defendant had committed a breach of contract claim. The plaintiff sought $80,000 in damages. Is the case properly removable?

A) Yes, because the parties are of diverse citizenship.

B) No, because the defendant is a citizen of the forum state.

C) Yes, because the claim is in excess of $75,000.

D) No, because the plaintiff is not a citizen of the forum state.

65. A California citizen living on the border with Arizona filed an action in Arizona state court against an Arizona citizen alleging that the defendant had violated his federally protected civil rights by refusing to rent him an apartment because of his race. The plaintiff sought $80,000 in damages. Is the case properly removable?

A) Yes, because the parties are of diverse citizenship.

B) No, because the defendant is a citizen of the forum state.

C) Yes, because the federal court has original jurisdiction over the claim.

D) No, because the plaintiff is not a citizen of the forum state.

66. A citizen of New Mexico filed a $400,000 tort claim in New Mexico state court against a Texas citizen. The day after the defendant received a copy of the complaint, he moved to New Mexico with the intention of staying there indefinitely. Is the case thereafter properly removable?

A) Yes, because the federal court has original jurisdiction over this claim under §1331.

B) Yes, because the federal court has original jurisdiction over this claim under §1332.

C) No, because the defendant became a citizen of the forum state.

D) No, because the federal court does not have original jurisdiction over this claim.

67. A Virginia citizen brought a $100,000 tort claim against a West Virginia citizen in a Virginia state court. After the defendant removed the case, the plaintiff amended her complaint to reduce her request for damages to $75,000. The plaintiff then filed a motion to remand. Should the court grant the motion?

A) No, because the defendant is not a citizen of the forum state.

B) Yes, because the claim is not in excess of $75,000.

C) No, because the federal court has original jurisdiction over this claim.

D) Yes, because plaintiff is a citizen of the forum state.

68. A Virginia citizen brought a $10,000 federal question claim against her former boss, a West Virginia citizen, in a Virginia state court. In that same suit, she also filed a $100,000 breach of contract claim against the local neighborhood grocery. Is the case properly removable?

A) No, because there is not complete diversity of citizenship between the adverse parties.

B) Yes, because her boss is not a citizen of the forum state.

C) Yes, because the breach of contract claim is for $100,000.

D) No, because the grocery store is a citizen of the forum state.

69. An Oregon citizen filed a lawsuit in Oregon state court asserting a $250,000 tort claim against an Idaho citizen and a $10,000 breach of contract claim against an Oregon citizen. Days after filing the complaint, the plaintiff voluntarily dismissed the claim against the Oregon defendant. The next day, the sole remaining defendant removed the case. Is the case properly removable?

A) Yes, because it now falls within the court's original jurisdiction.

B) No, because there is not complete diversity of citizenship.

C) Yes, because the plaintiff is a citizen of the forum state.

D) No, because the breach of contract claim is for $10,000.

70. An Oregon citizen filed a lawsuit in Oregon state court asserting a $250,000 tort claim against an Idaho citizen and a $10,000 breach of contract claim against an Oregon citizen. Two years after filing the complaint, while discovery is still being conducted, the plaintiff voluntarily dismissed the claim against the Oregon defendant. The next day, the sole remaining defendant removed the case. Is the case properly removable?

A) Yes, because it now falls within the court's original jurisdiction.

B) No, because the remaining defendant is a citizen of the forum state.

C) Yes, because the plaintiff is a citizen of the forum state.

D) No, because the dismissal of the Oregon defendant occurred two years after commencement of the litigation in state court.

71. A citizen of Utah filed an action in North Carolina state court asserting both a $500,000 tort claim against a Delaware citizen and a $100,000 breach of contract claim against a Utah citizen. The North Carolina court dismissed the claim against the Utah defendant on the ground that it did not have personal jurisdiction over that defendant. Is the case now properly removable?

A) No, because the remaining defendant is a citizen of the forum state.

B) Yes, because the federal court has original jurisdiction over the remaining claim.

C) No, because the nondiverse defendant was dismissed by a court order.

D) Yes, because the plaintiff is not a citizen of the forum state.

72. A citizen of Wyoming filed an action in Wyoming state court asserting a $300,000 breach of contract claim against another citizen of Wyoming. The defendant then filed a counterclaim alleging that the plaintiff had infringed the defendant's patent in violation of federal patent law. Is the case properly removable by the plaintiff?

A) No, because plaintiffs cannot remove cases.

B) Yes, because the federal court has original jurisdiction over the federal statutory counterclaim.

C) No, because the defendant is a citizen of the forum state.

D) Yes, because the plaintiff is a citizen of the forum state.

73. Following an accident, the driver and passenger of a car bring a tort action against the driver of the other car in state court in Texas. The plaintiff driver is a citizen of Texas and the passenger is a citizen of Louisiana. The defendant driver is a citizen of Texas. Each of the plaintiffs seeks $200,000 in damages against the defendant. The passenger also files a $200,000 claim against the driver of his car for damages resulting from the injury. Can that driver properly remove the case?

A) No, because plaintiffs cannot remove cases.

B) Yes, because the cross-claim meets all the requirements of §1332.

C) No, because the driver is a citizen of the forum state.

D) Yes, because the passenger is not a citizen of the forum state.

74. The purchaser of a defective refrigerator, a New Hampshire citizen, asserts a claim under the federal Consumer Protection Act for damages against the manufacturer, a New York citizen, as well as a $70,000 breach of contract action against a local printing shop that messed up the invitations to the plaintiff's upcoming wedding. This action is filed in New Jersey state court. Is the case properly removable?

A) No, because the plaintiff and the retailer are not diverse.

B) Yes, pursuant to §1441(c).

C) No, because the claim against the retailer is for $70,000.

D) Yes, because neither defendant is a citizen of the forum state.

75. A New York plaintiff filed an action in Pennsylvania state court asserting a $100,000 tort claim against a New Jersey citizen and an unrelated $10,000 breach of contract claim against a citizen of New York. Is the entire case properly removable?

A) Yes, because the two claims are separate and independent.

B) No, because there is not complete diversity of citizenship between the adverse parties.

C) Yes, because neither of the defendants are citizens of the forum state.

D) No, because the plaintiff is not a citizen of the forum state.

76. A Minnesota citizen filed a $100,000 claim in state court in Pennsylvania against a Pennsylvania mining company asserting violations of a collection of federal environmental statutes. His complaint also included a $100,000 claim against a Pennsylvania dredging company that, he alleged, operated alongside the mining company and committed violations of the state's environmental statutes. Is the entire case properly removable?

A) No, because the dredging company is a citizen of the forum state.

B) Yes, pursuant to §1441(c).

C) No, because the mining company is a citizen of the forum state.

D) Yes, because the plaintiff is not a citizen of the forum state.

77. A Florida manufacturer of a patented software product brought a claim in a Georgia state court alleging that a Georgia defendant was selling a pirated version of his software throughout the southern United States in violation of the federal patent statute. Assume that federal courts have exclusive subject matter jurisdiction over claims under the patent statute. Is the case properly removable?

A) No, because the state court did not have subject matter jurisdiction over the case.

B) Yes, because the federal court has original jurisdiction over the case.

C) No, because the defendant is a citizen of the forum state.

D) No, because the claim is not in excess of $75,000.

78. An Alabama citizen brought a $100,000 tort action in Alabama state court against a restaurant located in Hawaii alleging that the plaintiff had developed food poisoning while eating in that restaurant because of the unhygienic conditions present in the kitchen. The defendant removed the case. Thereafter, the restaurant filed a motion with the federal trial judge requesting that the court dismiss the case for lack of personal jurisdiction over it. The plaintiff acknowledges that the applicable long-arm statute does not provide jurisdiction over this defendant. Should the court grant this motion?

A) No, because by removing the case the defendant consented to that court's exercise of personal jurisdictional over it.

B) Yes, because the defendant is not subject to personal jurisdiction.

C) No, because the claim meets all the requirements of §1332.

D) Yes, because defendant is not a citizen of the forum state.

79. An Alabama citizen brought a $70,000 tort action in Alabama state court against a restaurant located in Hawaii alleging that he had developed food poisoning while eating in that restaurant because of the unhygienic conditions present in the kitchen. The defendant removed the case. Thereafter, the defendant filed a motion with the federal trial judge requesting that the court dismiss the case for lack of personal jurisdiction over it. The plaintiff acknowledges that the applicable long-arm statute does not provide jurisdiction over this defendant. Should the court grant this motion?

A) No, because by removing the case the defendant consented to that court's exercise of personal jurisdictional over it.

B) Yes, because the defendant is not subject to personal jurisdiction.

C) No, because the claim is for $70,000.

D) Yes, because the defendant is not a citizen of the forum state.

80. Sally, a resident of New York City, was vacationing in California when the taxi she was riding in collided with an automobile owned by Lou, a resident of San Francisco and driven by Sam, a resident of Los Angeles. Sally brought a tort action seeking $300,000 in damages against both Lou and Sam in the federal district court for the Central District of California, which is located in Los Angeles. San Francisco is located within the Northern District of California. Does venue lie in the chosen forum?

A) Yes, because the plaintiff chose this forum.

B) No, because the plaintiff is a resident of New York City.

C) Yes, because Sam resides there.

D) No, because Lou resides in San Francisco, which is located in the Northern District of California.

81. Sally, a resident of New York City, was vacationing in California when the taxi she was riding in collided with an automobile owned by Lou, a resident of San Francisco and driven by Sam, a resident of Los Angeles. Sally brought a tort action seeking $300,000 in damages against both Lou and Sam in the federal district court for the Southern District of New York, which is located in New York City. Does venue lie in the chosen forum?

A) Yes, because the plaintiff chose this forum.

B) No, because the plaintiff's residence is irrelevant for venue purposes and because the accident occurred and the defendants reside in California.

C) Yes, because the defendants are subject to personal jurisdiction in New York.

D) No, because New York law would govern the resolution of this case.

82. Jane went on a vacation to Europe with her two best friends, Leroy and Sally. Leroy is a resident of New York City and Sally is a resident of Chicago. Jane had been a lifelong resident of Chicago but moved to Philadelphia just before leaving for vacation. While they were in Paris, Leroy and Sally rented motorcycles and during their ride, they ran over Jane. Jane returned home and filed a civil action in federal court in Philadelphia asserting $200,000 tort claims against both Leroy and Sally. Neither Leroy nor Sally has ever been to Pennsylvania nor have either of them had any contact with the state. Does venue lie in the chosen forum?

A) No, because neither defendant resides there and the accident occurred in Paris.

B) Yes, because there is no other district in which venue would lie.

C) No, because Michigan law would govern the merits of the case.

D) Yes, because Jane is a resident of Philadelphia.

83. Jane went on a vacation to Hawaii with her best friend, Sally. Sally is a resident of Chicago. Jane had been a lifelong resident of Chicago but moved to Philadelphia just before leaving for vacation. While they were in Hawaii, Jane and Sally rented motorcycles and during their ride, Sally's motorcycle ran into Jane's motorcycle while Jane was on it. Jane returned home and filed a civil action in federal court in Philadelphia asserting $200,000 tort claims against Sally and Bike Rentals, Inc., the Hawaii rental company that is incorporated under the laws of Delaware. Sally has never been to Pennsylvania and never had any contact with the state. Although Bike Rentals, Inc. operates a highly interactive web site, no one in Pennsylvania has ever visited that site or purchased any products from the company. Does venue lie in the chosen forum?

A) Yes, because Jane is a resident of Philadelphia.

B) Yes, because the bike company is subject to personal jurisdiction in Pennsylvania.

C) No, neither of the defendants resides there and the accident occurred in Hawaii.

D) No, because Sally is not subject to personal jurisdiction in Pennsylvania.

84. Jane went on a vacation to Paris with her best friend, Sally. Sally is a resident of Chicago. Jane had been a lifelong resident of Chicago but moved to Philadelphia just before leaving for vacation. While they were in Paris, Jane and Sally rented motorcycles and during their ride, Sally's motorcycle ran into Jane's motorcycle while Jane was on it. Jane returned home and filed a civil action in federal court in Chicago asserting $200,000 tort claims against Sally and Pedalo, the motorcycle rental company in Paris. Does venue lie in the chosen forum?

A) Yes, because Sally resides there and Pedalo is a French company.

B) No, because Pedalo is a French company.

C) Yes, because Jane used to live in Chicago.

D) No, because the accident occurred in Paris.

85. A citizen of West Virginia brought a federal civil rights claim in a West Virginia state court against a police officer from Atlanta, Georgia, based on a beating the police officer gave the plaintiff while the plaintiff was vacationing in Atlanta. The defendant removed the case and then the plaintiff filed a motion to dismiss on the ground of improper venue. Should the court grant the motion?

A) Yes, because the events giving rise to the claim occurred in Georgia.

B) Yes, because the defendant resides in Georgia.

C) No, because the case was removed.

D) No, because the plaintiff resides in West Virginia.

86. A California plaintiff brought a $250,000 breach of contract action against an Arizona citizen in federal court in Phoenix. The complaint alleges that the defendant agreed to purchase $250,000 of merchandise from the defendant's store, shipped the merchandise to his home in Phoenix, and then refused to pay the invoice. The defendant moves to have the case transferred to the federal district court in Santa Fe, New Mexico. In his motion to transfer, the defendant declares that although he has no contacts with the state of New Mexico, he would waive any objections to personal jurisdiction and venue in that state. Should the court grant the motion to transfer?

A) Yes, because the defendant has waived his objections to jurisdiction and venue.

B) No, because the plaintiff would be subject to personal jurisdiction in New Mexico.

C) No, because New Mexico is not a district where this action might have been brought by the plaintiff.

D) Yes, because the plaintiff has no objection to the transfer.

87. A Texas plaintiff files a federal question claim against a Nevada defendant in federal district court in Houston. The events that gave rise to that action occurred exclusively in Nevada. The defendant has no contacts of any kind with Texas and so he moves to transfer the case under §1404 to the federal district court in Reno, Nevada. Should the court grant the motion?

A) No, because the Texas court does not have personal jurisdiction over the defendant.

B) Yes, because the action could have been brought in Reno and transfer there is in the interests of justice.

C) No, because venue does not lie in Houston.

D) Yes, under §1406.

88. A New York-incorporated and -based company brought a tort claim seeking $1 million in damages against a rival company based in Chicago and incorporated under the laws of Delaware. After being advised by its attorney that Texas law would be most hospitable to this claim, the plaintiff filed this action in a federal court in Dallas. None of the events that gave rise to this action were connected to Texas. Because it does business with customers all over the country, the defendant is subject to personal jurisdiction in many states, including Texas. The plaintiff subsequently moved to transfer the case to the district court in Chicago. Should the court grant this motion?

A) No, because plaintiffs cannot transfer cases under §1404.

B) Yes, because the action could have been brought in Chicago.

C) No, because this would allow the plaintiff to go forum shopping for the most advantageous law.

D) Yes, because the federal judges in Illinois can determine the content of Texas law.

89. A Texas citizen was given a two-year contract by a Saudi Arabian oil company to work in one of its plants in that country. After six months, the plaintiff was fired. She returned to America and filed a claim in federal court in Dallas against the Saudi company alleging that she was terminated on the basis of her sex in violation of Title VII of the federal Civil Rights Act of 1964. The defendant moved to dismiss the action on the ground that although it admitted that it was subject to personal jurisdiction in Texas because of its past business dealings there, maintaining the suit there would result in extreme inconvenience to it since all the alleged acts of discrimination occurred in Saudi Arabia, all the witnesses to the events in question were in Saudi Arabia, and defending in America would be extremely inconvenient. The plaintiff opposed the defense motion on the ground that a Saudi court would apply Saudi law to this dispute and that under Saudi law, she would have to establish malicious conduct beyond a reasonable doubt, whereas under Title VII, she would only have to prove negligent conduct by a preponderance of the evidence. Should the court dismiss the case?

A) Yes, under the doctrine of *forum non conveniens.*

B) No, because Saudi Arabian law is so hostile to the plaintiff's claim.

C) Yes, because the defendant is a foreign company.

D) No, because the plaintiff is an American citizen.

90. A Texas citizen was given a two-year contract by a Saudi Arabian oil company to work in one of its plants in that country. After six months, the plaintiff was fired. She returned to America and filed a claim in federal court in Dallas alleging that she was terminated on the basis of her sex in violation of Title VII of the federal Civil Rights Act of 1964. The defendant moved to dismiss the action on the ground that although it was subject to personal jurisdiction in Texas because of its past business dealings there, maintaining the suit there would result in extreme inconvenience to it since all the alleged acts of discrimination occurred in Saudi Arabia, all the witnesses to the events in question were in Saudi Arabia, and defending in America would be extremely inconvenient. The plaintiff opposed the defense motion on the ground that a Saudi court would apply Saudi law to this dispute and that Saudi law does not prohibit discrimination on the basis of sex. Should the court dismiss the case?

A) Yes, under the doctrine of *forum non conveniens.*

B) No, because under these circumstances dismissal would not further the interests of justice.

C) Yes, because the defendant is a foreign company.

D) No, because the plaintiff is an American citizen.

91. A Mississippi plaintiff brings a tort action against a California defendant in Mississippi state court. The Mississippi court grants the defense motion to dismiss on the ground that the defendant is not subject to personal jurisdiction in Mississippi. The plaintiff then brings precisely the same lawsuit against the same defendant in state court in California. The defendant moves to dismiss that action under the doctrine of claim preclusion. Should the court grant the motion?

A) Yes, because both lawsuits consist of the identical cause of action.

B) No, because the defendant is a citizen of California.

C) Yes, because the parties are the same in both lawsuits.

D) No, because the first dismissal did not constitute an adjudication on the merits.

92. A Mississippi plaintiff brings a tort action against a California defendant in California state court. The California court dismissed the complaint because the claim had expired under California's relatively short statute of limitations. The plaintiff then refiled the same claim in a Mississippi state court because Mississippi has a much longer statute of limitations. The defendant moves to dismiss the Mississippi action under the doctrine of claim preclusion. Should the court grant the motion?

A) Yes, because the parties are the same in both suits.

B) Yes, because the cause of action is the same in both suits.

C) No, because a dismissal for failing to file within the governing limitations period is not an adjudication on the merits distinguishing the claim.

D) No, because the plaintiff is a citizen of Mississippi.

93. Melvin Barrel was acquitted of a charge of bank robbery that had been filed against him in criminal court by the federal government. Shortly after his acquittal, Melvin was served with a civil complaint in which the government sought to recover possession of the money it alleged had been stolen by Melvin. Should the trial court in the civil case grant Melvin's motion to preclude relitigation of the issue of whether or not he stole the money from the bank?

A) No, because the parties to the two cases are not identical.

B) Yes, because this issue was already litigated in the previously concluded criminal case.

C) No, because the standard of proof is higher in criminal than in civil proceedings.

D) Yes, because the standard of proof is lower in civil than in criminal proceedings.

94. Melvin Barrel was convicted of a charge of bank robbery that had been filed against him in criminal court by the federal government. Shortly after his conviction, Melvin was served with a civil complaint in which the government sought to recover possession of the money it alleged had been stolen by Melvin. Should the trial court in the civil case grant the government's motion to preclude relitigation of the issue of whether or not Melvin stole the money from the bank?

A) No, because the parties to the two cases are not identical.

B) Yes, because the standard of proof is higher in criminal than in civil proceedings.

C) No, because the standard of proof is lower in civil than in criminal proceedings.

D) Yes, because the issue is the same in both cases.

Questions 95–99 are based on these facts:

Randy Costen, a citizen of Louisiana, filed an action in federal district court in New Orleans. His complaint contained a federal civil rights claim alleging that he had been the victim of unlawful sexual harassment and a breach of contract claim against his employer, Lasso, Inc., a citizen of Louisiana. The breach of contract claim alleged that Lasso had failed to pay Randy overtime as required by his employment contract. Costen also asserted a tort claim for intentional infliction of emotional distress against his boss, Shelly Martin, a citizen of Louisiana, alleging that it was her intentional acts of sexual harassment that caused him to suffer severe emotional distress. In addition to filing an answer, Lasso asserted a breach of contract claim against Costen and an indemnity claim against Shelly. In its breach of contract claim, Lasso alleged that Costen had not honored his contractual commitment to attend a variety of off-site conferences. Finally, Shelly responded to all of this by filing a third-party complaint against her insurance company, Worldwide Insurance, a citizen of Connecticut. In this complaint she asserted both a breach of contract claim alleging that the insurer had refused to pay a covered claim under her homeowner's policy and a state law claim for indemnity (under her professional liability policy) in connection with any liability she would incur as a result of Costen's cause of action against her.

95. Are all of Costen's claims against Lasso joinable?

A) No, because they do not arise out of the same transactions or occurrences.

B) Yes, because his right of joinder is unlimited.

C) No, because the parties are not diverse.

D) Yes, because the court has subject matter jurisdiction over both claims.

96. Is Costen's claim against Shelly joinable?

A) Yes, because his right of joinder is unlimited.

B) No, because Shelly and Costen are citizens of the same state.

C) Yes, because his claim against her arises out of the same occurrences that gave rise to his claim against Lasso and both claims contain a common question of fact.

D) No, because the court does not have subject matter jurisdiction over this claim.

97. Is Lasso's claim against Costen joinable?

A) Yes, because the right of joinder of counterclaims is unlimited.

B) No, because the parties are not diverse.

C) Yes, because the claim falls within the court's subject matter jurisdiction.

D) No, because the claims are not transactionally related.

98. Are Shelly's claims against Worldwide joinable?

A) Yes, as to the indemnity claim; no as to the contract claim.

B) No, as to both claims.

C) Yes, as to both claims.

D) Yes, as to the contract claim; no as to the indemnity claim.

99. Is Lasso's claim against Shelly joinable?

A) No, because the claim does not arise under federal law.

B) Yes, because its right of joinder is unlimited.

C) No, because the parties are citizens of the same state.

D) Yes, because this claim arises out of the transaction that gave rise to Costen's claim against Lasso.

100. Martin's Electronic Co., a Georgia citizen, brought a breach of contract action in federal court in Atlanta against its customer, Meredith Bane, a citizen of Florida, for failure to pay for the television that she purchased from its store in Atlanta. In her answer, Meredith admitted that she had not paid for the television but alleged that she had returned the television after she discovered its defective quality and refused to pay for it. The jury returned a verdict in favor of the defendant customer because it found that the defect breached the plaintiff's warranty of merchantability and so the defendant's refusal to pay was excused by the plaintiff's material breach of the sales contract. Some months later, Meredith filed a tort claim seeking damages in the amount of $70,000 against Martin's. In this complaint, Meredith alleged that when she turned on the television for the first time, it emitted sparks, which injured her and her property. The defendant moved to dismiss the claim on claim preclusion grounds. Should the court grant the motion?

A) Yes, because of the doctrine of defense preclusion.

B) No, because Meredith was a defendant in the first suit and the plaintiff in the second suit.

C) Yes, because the claim is for $70,000.

D) No, because the parties are citizens of different states.

Questions 101–110 are based on these facts:

Emily Landers, a lifelong resident of Atlanta, Georgia, brought suit in federal district court in Atlanta against a publisher, Ace Books, Inc., alleging copyright infringement under the federal copyright statute, for which she sought $100,000 in damages. Ace is incorporated under the laws of Delaware and has its principal place of business in New York City. Emily also filed a claim against Ace alleging that it had breached its agreement with her to publish her book upon receipt of a manuscript. She sought $60,000 in damages in connection with that claim. In that same suit, Emily also filed a $105,000 tort claim against the president of Ace, Gordon Jackson, a citizen of New York, alleging that he had intentionally inflicted emotional distress upon her by sending emails to dozens of other publishers denouncing her as a horrible writer and a fraud and explaining that those were the reasons for his company's refusal to publish her book. In this same action, Ace filed a claim against Jackson seeking indemnity for any liability it might accrue in connection with

Emily's copyright infringement claim against it. In response, Jackson filed a breach of contract claim against Ace alleging that Ace had improperly withheld two weeks of salary from him totaling $65,000. Finally, Jackson asserted a tort claim against his neighbor, Sue, claiming that her negligent maintenance of her home significantly depreciated the value of his property, for which he sought an injunction and $45,000 in damages.

101. Can the court exercise subject matter jurisdiction over both of Emily's claims against Ace?

    A) No, because she sought only $60,000 in damages with respect to the breach of contract claim.

    B) No, because copyright claims fall within the exclusive subject matter jurisdiction of the federal courts.

    C) Yes, under the combination of §§1331 and 1441.

    D) Yes, under the combination of §§1331 and 1332.

102. Can the court exercise subject matter jurisdiction over Emily's claim against Jackson?

    A) Yes, under §1367.

    B) Yes, under §1441.

    C) Yes, under §1332.

    D) No, because Jackson and Ace are citizens of the same state.

103. Can the court exercise subject matter jurisdiction over Ace's claim against Jackson?

    A) Yes, under §1367(a).

    B) Yes, under §1367(b).

    C) No, because of §1367(b).

    D) No, because Jackson is not diverse from Ace.

104. Is Ace's claim against Jackson joinable?

    A) No, because the parties are nondiverse.

    B) Yes, because it is an indemnity claim.

    C) Yes, because there is no limit to joinability of such claims.

    D) No, because there has been no showing that Jackson has any contacts with the forum state.

105. Is Emily's breach of contract claim against Ace joinable?

    A) Yes, because there is no limit to joinability of such claims.

    B) No, because it is not a claim for indemnity.

    C) Yes, because the parties are diverse and the claim meets the amount in controversy requirement.

    D) No, because Ace is not a citizen of the forum state.

106. Can the court exercise subject matter jurisdiction over Jackson's breach of contract claim against Ace?

    A) No, because Jackson and Ace are citizens of New York.

    B) Yes, because Ace is a citizen of Delaware.

    C) No, because it is unrelated to the copyright claim.

    D) No, because the breach did not occur in Georgia.

107. Is Jackson's breach of contract claim against Ace joinable?

    A) Yes, because there is no limit to joinability of this type of claim.

    B) No, because it is unrelated to the events that gave rise to Ace's claim against Jackson.

    C) Yes, because Ace was named in the complaint.

    D) No, because the parties are not diverse.

108. Is Jackson's claim against Sue joinable?

    A) Yes, because Jackson was a named defendant.

    B) No, because these two parties are citizens of the same state.

    C) Yes, because it is a complaint for indemnity.

    D) No, because it is a tort claim alleging conduct that lowered the value of his property.

109. Can the court exercise subject matter jurisdiction over Jackson's claim against Sue?

    A) No, because the claim is for $45,000.

    B) No, because Jackson is seeking an injunction.

    C) No, because neither Jackson nor Sue are citizens of Georgia.

    D) No, because this claim seeks relief from Sue's maintenance of her property.

110. Is Jackson a properly joined defendant in this case?

A) No, because he is not a citizen of Georgia.

B) Yes, because he is a citizen of a different state than Emily.

C) Yes, because this claim is transactionally related to Emily's claim against Ace and the two claims share a common question of fact.

D) Yes, because the claim is for $105,000.

Questions 111–115 are based on these facts:

Sam is injured in a crash between his car and another car and a truck on a narrow country road in Concord, New Hampshire. Sam is a citizen of New Hampshire. The driver of the other car, Karen, is a citizen of Maine, and the owner of the truck, Ace Trucking, is incorporated under the laws of Delaware and has its principal place of business in Connecticut. Sam files an action in the federal court for the District of New Hampshire seeking damages of $250,000 against each of the two named defendants, Karen and Ace. In the same suit, Karen files a claim against Ace seeking $75,000 in damages for the damage to her car. Ace files a tort claim against Sam seeking $70,000 in damages for the damages to its truck. Ace also files a claim against Barbara, a citizen of Connecticut who was driving its truck at the time of the accident, seeking indemnity from any loss it might suffer in connection with Sam's claim against it.

111. Can the court exercise subject matter jurisdiction over Karen's claim against Ace?

A) Yes, because Karen and Ace are citizens of different states.

B) No, because she is seeking $70,000.

C) Yes, because this claim arose out of the car crash.

D) No, because original jurisdiction was based solely on diversity.

112. Can the court exercise subject matter jurisdiction over Ace's claim against Sam?

A) Yes, because Ace and Sam are citizens of different states.

B) No, because Ace is seeking $70,000.

C) Yes, because this claim arose out of the car crash.

D) No, because original jurisdiction was based solely on diversity.

113. Can the court exercise subject matter jurisdiction over Ace's claim against Barbara?

A) No, because Ace and Barbara are citizens of the same state.

B) Yes, because Barbara is not a citizen of Georgia.

C) Yes, because this claim arose out of the car crash.

D) No, because original jurisdiction was based solely on diversity.

114. Does venue lie over Sam's claim against Karen?

A) Yes, because the parties are diverse.

B) Yes, because Sam resides in New Hampshire.

C) No, because none of the defendants reside in New Hampshire.

D) Yes, because the accident occurred in New Hampshire.

115. Does venue lie over Ace's claim against Barbara?

A) No, because Barbara does not reside in New Hampshire

B) No, because Ace and Barbara are not diverse.

C) Yes, because this is a third-party claim.

D) Yes, because this claim arose out of the same nucleus of fact that gave rise to Sam's claim against Ace.

CIVIL PROCEDURE
MULTIPLE CHOICE
ANSWERS & ANALYSIS

> ## CIVIL PROCEDURE ANSWERS AND ANALYSIS

1. Issue: Constitutionality of personal jurisdiction

The correct answer is **A**. The proper approach to determining whether or not a state court can exercise personal jurisdiction is a two-step analysis. First, one must determine whether the applicable state long-arm statute applies. Here, the fact that Acadia is doing more than $3 million in annual business with New York customers, both those that come to New Orleans and bring the whiskey to New York and those who buy it over the Internet. So the statute applies. One must then determine the constitutionality of exercising jurisdiction. That is a multi-step process. First, is the court attempting to exercise specific or general jurisdiction? The question asks only for specific jurisdiction, which means that the cause of action arises out of the defendant's relationships with the forum state. Here, the cause of action is for damages caused by the defective product. While it could be argued that the defendant's connection with the forum are only the transport and not the manufacture of the product, if one views the connection as the entire business of producing and distributing liquor, then the cause of action does arise out of the defendant's relationships with the forum. In that case, one must then evaluate the extent of the defendant's relationship. Since this appears to be a continuous and systematic relationship, the *International Shoe* standard is met. One must then also evaluate the "fairness" factors set forth in *Volkswagen*. Here, the plaintiff is a forum citizen and so both he and the forum state have an interest in having the case heard in the chosen forum. And the interstate judicial system has an interest in having the case heard in New York since lots of the witnesses including the plaintiff and his doctors are in the forum. Consequently, A is the correct answer. Answer B is incorrect because the cause of action would not arise out of those contacts (the bank account) and so this could not be the exercise of specific jurisdiction. Answer C is incorrect because the long-arm statute does not require the tortious act to have been committed in New York. It permits jurisdiction where the defendant commits a tortious act outside the forum but causes injury inside the forum, which happened here. Answer D is incorrect because Acadia clearly has extensive contacts with New York.

2. Issue: Constitutionality of personal jurisdiction

The correct answer is **D**. State courts have personal jurisdiction over their citizens, even if they are not residing in the forum state at the time suit is brought. There is no need to examine the application of the long-arm statute since these statutes deal with obtaining personal jurisdiction over noncitizens and nonresidents. There is also no constitutional objection to exercising personal jurisdiction over a forum citizen. Consequently, all the other answers are incorrect.

3. Issue: Constitutionality of personal jurisdiction

The correct answer is **D**. In a *quasi in rem* proceeding, the defendant must have property within the forum state, the property must not be the subject of the plaintiff's claim, and, under the Court's ruling in *Shaffer*, the exercise of jurisdiction must meet constitutional requirements. Here, the first two portions of this standard are clearly met. With respect to the constitutional inquiry, one must evaluate the extent of the defendant's relationship with the forum state to see if it supports this attempt to exercise general jurisdiction. Because the defendant conducts extensive other business in the forum state, besides dealing with its bank account, this level of relationship or contacts is extensive enough to justify the exercise of general jurisdiction. And the *Volkswagen* "fairness" factors also support jurisdiction since the plaintiff (as a forum citizen) and the forum state have an interest in having the case adjudicated in New York and much of the evidence is located there. Answers A and B are incorrect because they are irrelevant to fulfilling the statutory requirement for exercising *quasi in rem* jurisdiction, which requires the presence of defendant's property within the forum. Answer C is incorrect because it suggests that the mere presence of the defendant's property in the forum state is sufficient. The Supreme Court in *Shaffer* held that this is no longer the case; an exercise of *quasi in rem* jurisdiction must also pass constitutional scrutiny.

4. Issue: General jurisdiction

The correct answer is **D**. Acadia does have some contacts with these states because it is doing some business there. But the plaintiff's cause of action does not arise out of these relationships and so the court would have to have general jurisdiction over Acadia. This would require a more significant degree of relationship than is suggested by the facts of this case. That is why D is the best answer. It is true that Acadia does not have a bank account in these states, but that is not why those states cannot exercise specific jurisdiction over it, which is why A is not correct. The mere fact that Acadia does business in these states is not enough, in itself, to justify this attempt at exercising specific jurisdiction. One would have to evaluate the extent of that business and the extent is insufficient to justify general jurisdiction since only 5% of its sales are made to citizens of those two states. Therefore, B is not a correct answer. It is also true that Acadia did not commit a tortious act in these states but that is not why they cannot exercise general jurisdiction over it. Therefore, D is also incorrect.

5. Issue: Federal court personal jurisdiction

The correct answer is **D**. Federal Rule of Civil Procedure 4(k)(1) provides that in the absence of a governing federal statute, the federal court applies the state long-arm statute of the forum state. Since this is a tort claim governed by state law, there is no applicable federal long-arm provision and so the forum's long-arm statute applies. No other factor is relevant, which is why the other answers are incorrect.

6. Issue: Tag jurisdiction

The correct answer is **D**. The Supreme Court ruled in *Burnham* that personal service in the forum state, so-called tag jurisdiction, is constitutionally sufficient. In such cases, there is no need to investigate the fairness of exercising jurisdiction because in-state service, the plurality ruled in *Burnham*, meets the due process test of fairness. Thus, answers A and C are incorrect. Answer B is incorrect because the citizenship of the plaintiff is irrelevant to the constitutional assessment required by *Shoe* with respect to the existence of personal jurisdiction over the defendant.

7. Issue: Federal court personal jurisdiction

The correct answer is **D**. Under Fed. R. Civ. P. 4(k)(1), a federal court looks to the forum state's jurisdictional provision unless otherwise provided by federal law. Here, the substantive federal law contains its own jurisdictional provision. Consequently, it, rather than state law, applies.

8. Issue: Federal court personal jurisdiction

The correct answer is **C**. Since, under Fed. R. Civ. P. 4(k)(1), the jurisdictional provision contained in the federal antitrust law applies, the constitutionality of the exercise of such jurisdiction must be determined under the Fifth Amendment. Under that analysis, as opposed to Fourteenth Amendment analysis that applies when the case is governed by a state jurisdictional provision, we look to the defendant's contacts with the United States as a whole rather than with the forum state. Thus, answer A is wrong because the Fourteenth Amendment is inapposite. Answer B is wrong because it focuses on the defendant's contacts with the forum state. Answer D is wrong because there is a constitutional limitation upon the exercise of personal jurisdiction by federal district courts.

9. Issue: Pendent personal jurisdiction

The correct answer is **D**. The issue here is whether the fact that the defendant would not be subject to personal jurisdiction with respect to one of the claims, here the state law claim, precludes the court from exercising jurisdiction over it with respect to the entire case. Borrowing the concept from subject matter jurisdiction law, the courts are beginning to recognize a doctrine of pendent personal jurisdiction over a defendant where there is a federal claim against the defendant that falls within the court's personal jurisdiction and a state law claim that arises out of the same nucleus of events that gave rise to the federal law claim. Here, then, the doctrine of pendent personal jurisdiction is in play. But since the state law claim arises out of "an unrelated matter" from the event giving rise to the federal claim, the two claims do not constitute one "case," i.e., they do not arise out of a common nucleus of operative fact. Hence, the court would not apply the doctrine of pendent personal jurisdiction and the state law claim would have to be dismissed.

10. Issue: Sufficiency of service of process in federal court

The correct answer is **C**. Under Fed. R. Civ. P. 4(e)(1), in civil actions filed in federal court, service must be made either pursuant to governing federal law, the state statute of the forum state or the state in which service is effected, or the specific provisions of Rule 4(e)(2) of the Federal Rules of Civil Procedure. Since this claim was not filed under a federal statute containing its own service provision, and none of the answers direct us to Rule 4(e)(2), we must look to the state law of either the forum or the state in which service is made. Since Alabama law is not mentioned as an answer, the correct answer is C since service is sought to be effected in New York.

11. Issue: "Residing therein" under Fed. R. Civ. P. 4(e)(2)(B)

The correct answer is **D**. Under Fed. R. Civ. P. 4(e)(2)(B), service is sufficient if it is delivered to the defendant's dwelling house or usual place of abode with some person of suitable age and discretion "then residing therein." Since the housekeeper does not live in the defendant's home, this latter requirement has not been met. While some courts have said that this defect can be cured by the fact that the defendant actually receives the notice, this defendant did not receive the process.

12. Issue: "Dwelling house" under Fed. R. Civ. P. 4(e)(2)(B)

The correct answer is **B**. This assumes that the house is the defendant's "dwelling house or usual place of abode." Under Fed. R. Civ. P. 4(e)(2)(B), service is sufficient if it is delivered to the defendant's "dwelling house or usual place of abode" with some person of suitable age and discretion then residing therein. Here, the defendant owns many homes. The courts have concluded that a defendant can have more than one dwelling house or usual place of abode. A home will fit this bill if there are indicia of permanence such as the presence of furnishings or other manifestations of repeated presence. Assuming that this standard has been met, the other requirements of the Rule have also been met. Answer A is wrong because the fact that the defendant was not personally served nor was present at the time of service is not fatal. Answer C is incorrect because the courts have ruled that as long as the formal requirements of service have been met, actual receipt by the defendant is not required. Answer D is incorrect because the mere fact that you serve a defendant's wife is not enough to meet the requirements of Rule 4(e)(2)(B).

13. Issue: "Agent authorized by appointment" under Fed. R. Civ. P. 4(e)(2)(C)

The correct answer is **B**. Under Fed. R. Civ. P. 4(e)(2)(C), service can be made upon an agent authorized by appointment to receive service of process. Thus, the fact that she was not served at the defendant's home is not fatal and so answers C and D are incorrect. The issue here is whether the defendant's attorney meets that test, i.e., whether the attorney was appointed for the purpose of receiving service of process. The courts have held that the mere existence of a prior attorney/client relationship is not sufficient to deem the attorney the agent for service of process purposes. Thus, answer A is incorrect. There needs to be some manifestation of intent on the client's part to permit the attorney to receive process. Absent an express declaration of that intent, the court might look to whether the attorney had been authorized to receive service in a prior representation.

14. Issue: "Agent authorized by appointment" under Fed. R. Civ. P. 4(e)(2)(C)

The correct answer is **A**. Under Fed. R. Civ. P. 4(e)(2)(C), service can be made upon an agent authorized by appointment to receive service of process. The Supreme Court in *National Equipment Rental v. Szukhent* held that a service provision in a form contract can constitute an effective appointment of an agent for service of process even if the recipient is unknown to the plaintiff. The only requirement of the job is to transfer service to the defendant and if that job is fulfilled, the Court ruled, the service is effective. That occurred here and so the service is proper under Rule 4(e)(2)(C). The defects alluded to in answers B and C are irrelevant under these circumstances, as is the fact offered in answer D.

15. Issue: Constitutional sufficiency of service

The correct answer is **C**. In *Mullane*, the Supreme Court held that the due process requirements of the Fourteenth Amendment must be applied to determine the constitutional sufficiency of notice regardless of whether the proceeding is deemed to be *in personam, in rem,* or *quasi in rem*. Thus, although this is an *in rem* case, mere seizure plus publication no longer is always constitutionally sufficient. Thus, answers A, B, and D are incorrect. The constitutional requirement for notice is that notice which is reasonably calculated under all the circumstances to apprise interested parties of the pendency of the action. Since the defendant's whereabouts were known to the plaintiff, the ruling in *Mullane* would require more than publication—the plaintiff would have to mail service to the defendant's known home address.

16. Issue: Well pleaded complaint rule

The correct answer is **B**. While it is true that the parties are not of diverse citizenship, the court would have federal question jurisdiction under §1331 if the federal question met the well pleaded complaint rule, i.e., the federal question was part of the plaintiff's prima facie case. Thus, answer D is incorrect. This is a basic breach of contract claim by the plaintiff. The federal issue concerning the federal disclosure statute comes into the case only as a defense issue and therefore the federal question is not part of a well pleaded complaint. Thus, it does not arise under federal law under §1331 and so answer A is incorrect. Objections to subject matter jurisdiction can never be waived and so answer C is incorrect.

17. Issue: Well pleaded complaint rule

The correct answer is **B**. While it is true that the parties are not of diverse citizenship, the court would have federal question jurisdiction under §1331 if the federal question met the well pleaded complaint rule, i.e., the federal question was part of the plaintiff's prima facie case. Thus, answer D is incorrect because it does not go far enough. This is a basic breach of contract claim by the plaintiff. Although a federal constitutional issue is raised in the plaintiff's complaint, it is only there as a response to an anticipated federal defense. Thus, it is not deemed to have arisen within a well pleaded complaint. Consequently, it does not arise under federal law under §1331 and so answer A is incorrect. Objections to subject matter jurisdiction can never be waived and so answer C is incorrect.

18. Issue: Jurisdictional amount in controversy

The correct answer is **D**. Unlike diversity cases, there is no jurisdictional amount in controversy requirement for federal question cases under §1331. Thus, answer A is incorrect. The fact that the parties are diverse does not provide a basis for jurisdiction under §1332 because that would require an amount in controversy in excess of $75,000, which is not present here. Thus, answer C is incorrect. The case clearly arises under federal law and so answer B is incorrect.

19. Issue: Concurrent jurisdiction over federal question claims

The correct answer is **B**. The question here is whether a state court would have subject matter jurisdiction over a federal statutory claim. State courts have concurrent jurisdiction over claims arising under all federal statutes except those few that vest federal courts with exclusive jurisdiction. The Civil Rights Act is not one of those few statutes. All of the other answers are wrong because they relate to the subject matter jurisdiction of a federal, and not a state court. Answer C is not correct because it does not go far enough. The fact that a claim arises under federal law does not always mean that the state court has subject matter jurisdiction because some minority of federal statutes provide for exclusive jurisdiction in the federal courts. Answer D is incorrect because there is no amount in controversy requirement for federal claims being heard in state court.

20. Issue: Master of the complaint rule

The correct answer is **B**. As the master of the complaint, the plaintiff is permitted to choose which claims to assert and not assert. Assuming that a well pleaded state law claim does not contain a substantial issue of federal law, as this would not, then the plaintiff can refuse to assert the federal claim to avoid having the defendant remove the case. Thus, the fact that the plaintiff could state a federal claim is irrelevant and, therefore, answer A is incorrect. There is an exception to the master of the complaint doctrine, the so-called artful pleading doctrine. This states that when the plaintiff's purported state law claim is "really" a federal law claim, it must be treated as a federal claim for subject matter jurisdictional purposes. But this occurs only when the purported state law claim asserts a right to relief in a subject that has been preempted by state law. The field of antidiscrimination law is not one in which federal law preempts any effort at state regulation. Therefore, answer C is incorrect since the master of the complaint doctrine is, by itself, not a complete answer. The fact that the parties are not diverse would not preclude federal jurisdiction if the plaintiff's claim was "really" a federal claim and so answer D is incorrect.

21. Issue: Definition of citizenship for a natural person

The correct answer is **A**. Since this is a state law claim, jurisdiction is only available under §1332, which requires diversity of citizenship. Citizenship for a natural person has been construed by the courts to mean domicile. The defendant was domiciled in North Dakota at least until she moved to Illinois. The question therefore is whether she changed her domicile to Illinois. To establish a change of domicile, the defendant must be both physically present in a new location and manifest an intention to remain there indefinitely. Since the defendant has not indicated any intention to remain in Illinois, but, to the contrary, has expressed an intention to return to North Dakota upon finishing her studies, she remains a domiciliary, and thus a citizen, of North Dakota. Therefore, the parties are of diverse citizenship and the amount in controversy exceeds $75,000. Since both diversity and the amount in controversy must be present, answer D is incorrect. Since the defendant is a citizen of North Dakota, answer B is incorrect. Residence is an irrelevant concept for diversity purposes. The touchstone is domicile, not residence.

22. Issue: Corporate citizenship

The correct answer is **B**. Corporate citizenship for diversity purposes is defined in §1332(c) as both the state of incorporation and the state of the corporation's principal place of business. Since the defendant's headquarters and warehouse are located in Utah, its principal place of business is in Utah. Therefore, it is a citizen of Utah. So is the plaintiff. The fact that the defendant is also a citizen of Delaware because it is incorporated there is irrelevant. The parties are not diverse. So answer A is incorrect. The fact that the defendant is a citizen of the forum state is irrelevant to diversity of citizenship jurisdiction under §1332. It may preclude removal under §1441(b), but this was not a removed case, so that is irrelevant. Thus, answer C is incorrect. Answer D is incorrect because the extent of Early Bird's contacts with the forum state is relevant to personal, but not subject matter jurisdiction.

23. Issue: Complete diversity requirement

The correct answer is **B**. The Supreme Court has interpreted the diversity of citizenship requirement contained in §1332 to require complete diversity between adverse parties. So the plaintiff must be diverse from both defendants. Although the plaintiff and Simon are diverse, the plaintiff and Early Bird are both citizens of Utah since Utah is the state of Early Bird's principal place of business. Therefore, there is not complete diversity of citizenship. Thus, A is incorrect because it is irrelevant; C is wrong because it is not sufficient to satisfy the jurisdictional amount in controversy requirement if the parties are not diverse and the claim is under state law; and D is incorrect because the suit does not have to be filed in the corporate defendant's state of incorporation in terms of the requirements for subject matter jurisdiction.

24. Issue: Complete diversity requirement

Answer **C** is the correct answer. The fact that one plaintiff and one defendant are both citizens of the same foreign country is irrelevant for the purposes of determining the existence of diversity of citizenship. Thus, answer B is incorrect. The requirement of complete diversity under §1332(a)(1) does not require that aliens who are adverse parties from one another be citizens of different countries. The reason there is no diversity jurisdiction is because both the plaintiff Sheila and defendant Early Bird are citizens of Utah and, therefore, they are not diverse and so there is no complete diversity between the plaintiffs and the defendants. Answer A is incorrect because aliens can invoke federal jurisdiction under §1332(a)(2). Answer D is incorrect because it is not sufficient to satisfy the jurisdictional amount in controversy requirement if the parties to a state law claim are not diverse.

25. Issue: Citizenship of dual national

The correct answer is **B**. Individuals with dual nationality, one of which is American, cannot invoke §1332(a)(2) alienage jurisdiction. They are always considered American citizens for those purposes. Since the defendant is domiciled in Texas, he is also a citizen of Texas. So is the plaintiff. Therefore the parties are not diverse and since this is not a federal question claim, the court would not have subject matter jurisdiction. Answer A is incorrect because a dual national with American citizenship cannot invoke alienage jurisdiction. Answer C is wrong because aliens can invoke federal jurisdiction or be sued in federal court if the requirements of §1332(a)(2) are satisfied. Answer D is incorrect because it is not sufficient to satisfy the jurisdictional amount in controversy requirement if the parties to a state law claim are not diverse.

26. Issue: Citizenship of dual national

The correct answer is **B**. Individuals with dual nationality, one of which is American, cannot invoke §1332(a)(2) alienage jurisdiction. Therefore, answer A is incorrect. The only possibility is diversity jurisdiction under §1332(a)(1). The defendant is an American citizen but since he is permanently domiciled in Paris, he is not domiciled in any state in the United States and therefore is not a citizen of any state of the United States. Therefore, he cannot be made subject to diversity jurisdiction under §1332(a)(1). That is why answer B is the correct answer. Had the defendant been domiciled in any state in the United States other than Virginia, the parties would be diverse. Answer C is incorrect because it is not sufficient to satisfy the jurisdictional amount in controversy requirement if the parties to a state law claim are not diverse. Answer D is incorrect because the extent of the defendant's contacts with the forum state is relevant to personal, but not subject matter jurisdiction.

27. Issue: Assignment of claims and collusive joinder

The correct answer is **B**. 28 U.S.C. §1359 states that a district court will not have subject matter jurisdiction when a party has been collusively joined for the purpose of invoking that court's subject matter jurisdiction. The question, therefore, is whether the assignment to the New Yorker was made by the original claimholder for the purpose of creating diversity-based jurisdiction. This turns on whether the original claimholder/assignor retained an interest in the claim or where other aspects of the assignment indicate that it was made solely for the purpose of invoking federal jurisdiction. Since, in this case, the original claimholder gave up all interest in the claim for a reasonable amount of money, it is clear that this was not a collusive assignment within the meaning of §1359. Thus, since the defendant and (New York) plaintiff are diverse and the claim is in excess of $75,000, there is jurisdiction under §1332(a)(1). Thus, answers A and C are incorrect. The fact that the plaintiff is a citizen of the forum state is irrelevant to this question and so answer D is incorrect.

28. Issue: Assignment of claims and collusive joinder

The correct answer is **B**. 28 U.S.C. §1359 states that a district court will not have subject matter jurisdiction when a party has been collusively joined for the purpose of invoking that court's subject matter jurisdiction. The question, therefore, is whether the assignment to the New Yorker was made by the original claimholder for the purpose of creating diversity-based jurisdiction. This turns on whether the original claimholder/assignor retained an interest in the claim or where other aspects of the assignment indicate that it was made solely for the purpose of invoking federal jurisdiction. Since, in this case, the original claimholder retained all of his interest in the claim and only paid the putative plaintiff a service fee, the courts would find this to be a collusive joinder and disregard the citizenship of the assignee. Therefore, answers A and C are incorrect. Since the citizenship of the original claimholder would govern, the parties are not diverse. Answer D is incorrect because the fact that the defendant is a citizen of the forum state is irrelevant to this question.

29. Issue: Assignment of claims and collusive joinder

The correct answer is **A**. The trick here is that the assignment, if collusive in intention, was made for the purpose of defeating diversity jurisdiction. Section 1359 expressly applies only to collusive joinder for the purpose of invoking federal jurisdiction. Nevertheless, the federal courts have construed §1359 to apply to collusive joinder to both invoke and defeat jurisdiction. Thus, §1359 would apply here if the assignment was collusive. Since the original claimholder retained all real interest in the claim minus a service fee, the assignment was collusive. Thus, the original claimholder's citizenship governs and there is diversity jurisdiction since the state law claim is for $100,000. Thus, answers B, C, and D are incorrect.

30. Issue: Complete diversity requirement

The correct answer is **C**. A state law claim can be heard in federal court if the requirements of §1332 are met and so answer D is incorrect. The diversity requirement only applies to the citizenship of the adverse parties. The fact that co-parties, as in this case, are not diverse from one another is irrelevant for §1332 purposes. Therefore, answer A is incorrect. The fact that the defendants are citizens of the forum state is irrelevant since this case was not removed, but was originally filed in federal court. Therefore, answer B is incorrect.

31. Issue: Citizenship of permanent resident alien

The correct answer is **B**. Under the final provision of §1332(a), an alien who is lawfully admitted to the United States for permanent residence is deemed a citizen of the state in which the alien is domiciled. The courts have construed this to mean that such an alien cannot invoke alienage jurisdiction under §1332(a)(2). Thus, answer A is incorrect. This means that under the facts of this problem, the defendant is domiciled in Washington and thus is a citizen of Washington, as is the plaintiff. Therefore, the parties are not diverse. Answer C is thus incorrect because it is not sufficient to meet the amount in controversy requirement when the parties are not diverse. Answer D is an incorrect statement of the law.

32. Issue: Aggregation of value of diversity claims

The correct answer is **C**. Since the plaintiff and defendant are diverse, the issue is whether a single plaintiff can aggregate the value of claims against a single defendant to meet the jurisdictional amount in controversy requirement for diversity cases. The answer is yes. Therefore, answer D is incorrect. Answer A is incorrect because the fact of diversity alone is insufficient to invoke §1332 jurisdiction. You need to satisfy the amount in controversy requirement as well. The fact that the defendant is a citizen of the forum state is irrelevant and, therefore, answer B is incorrect.

33. Issue: Aggregation of value of diversity claims

The correct answer is **B**. Since the plaintiff is diverse from both defendants, the issue is whether a single plaintiff can aggregate the value of claims against multiple defendants to meet the jurisdictional amount in controversy requirement for diversity cases. The answer to this is no. While multiple claims brought by a single plaintiff against a single defendant can be aggregated, the courts do not permit aggregation of claims by a single plaintiff against multiple defendants. Thus, since the claim against neither defendant independently meets the jurisdictional amount requirement, answer C is incorrect. Answer A is incorrect because diversity without the proper amount in controversy is not enough for §1332 jurisdiction. Federal courts can hear claims under state law if the requirements of §1332 are met and therefore answer D is incorrect.

34. Issue: Jurisdictional amount in controversy

The correct answer is **B**. A single plaintiff cannot aggregate the value of claims against multiple defendants to meet the jurisdictional amount in controversy requirement for diversity cases. But here the amount of each claim is $75,000. But §1332(a)(1) requires that the amount in controversy "exceed the value or sum of $75,000." Each claim against the separate defendants must be independently evaluated and since each such claim is only for exactly $75,000, neither claim is in excess of $75,000. Therefore, the amount in controversy requirement has not been satisfied. Thus, answer C is incorrect. Answer A is incorrect because diversity without the proper amount in controversy is not enough for §1332 jurisdiction. Federal courts can hear claims under state law if the requirements of §1332 are met and therefore answer D is incorrect.

35. Issue: Aggregation of value of diversity claims

The correct answer is **D**. The claims of multiple plaintiffs against a common defendant cannot be aggregated to meet the jurisdictional amount in controversy requirement. Therefore, since neither individual claim exceeds $75,000, the amount in controversy requirement has not been met. Thus, answer C is incorrect. Answer A is incorrect because diversity without the proper amount in controversy is not enough for §1332 jurisdiction. Answer B is incorrect because the fact that the defendants are citizens of the forum state is irrelevant to this problem.

36. Issue: Jurisdictional amount in controversy

The correct answer is **C**. The issue here is whether the fact that the verdict was for less than $75,000 is relevant to the court's exercise of subject matter jurisdiction. Section 1332(b) provides that where the plaintiff recovers less than $75,000, the court can deny costs to the plaintiff and impose costs on the plaintiff. At the same time, §1332(a) requires that the matter "in controversy" in diversity cases exceed $75,000. The courts interpret the latter requirement merely to demand that the amount placed in controversy by the plaintiff's complaint exceed $75,000. (There is an exception to this rule if it can be determined pre-trial that the plaintiff could not recover in excess of $75,000 to a legal certainty.) If the plaintiff ultimately recovers less than that amount, it does not deprive the court of jurisdiction, it merely provides the court with the opportunity to shift costs to the plaintiff. Answer A is incorrect because objections to subject matter jurisdiction can never be waived. Answer B is incorrect because the amount in controversy requirement is met. Answer D is incorrect because the fact that the defendant is a citizen of the forum state is irrelevant to this problem.

37. Issue: Jurisdictional amount in controversy

The correct answer is **C**. The courts uniformly employ a rebuttable presumption that the face of the complaint is a good faith representation of the actual amount in controversy. Flowing from this rule that the amount in controversy is to be assessed by looking at the face of the plaintiff's complaint and the time of its filing (unless the party opposing the exercise of jurisdiction can rebut the presumption by persuading the court "to a legal certainty" that the amount recoverable cannot meet the jurisdictional threshold) is the corollary that the amount contained on the face of the complaint cannot be whittled down by a consideration of any affirmative defense asserted on the merits. The idea here is that since an affirmative defense is not contained in the plaintiff's complaint, consideration of the impact of merit-based affirmative defenses on the jurisdictional question of the amount in controversy would force the court to wait until the answer is filed to see if the affirmative defense is asserted. That is because, among other things, affirmative defense are waivable and so if the defendant fails to assert them, they are lost. Moreover, the courts are leery of assessing any issue going to the merits of the case in determining the jurisdictional threshold question. To do otherwise would subject assessments of jurisdiction to repeated review throughout the conduct of the trial. Consequently, the courts find that face-of-the-complaint-when-filed rule precludes the consideration of waivable affirmative defenses in determining whether the amount in controversy has been met.

In this hypothetical, the defendant is alleging that under the doctrine of preclusion, the jury's finding in case #1 precludes any possibility of relief beyond that associated with the damages for injuries not considered in that case, i.e., $50,000. Since that amount clearly does not meet the jurisdictional threshold, it is argued, the court cannot exercise diversity jurisdiction. The courts have rejected this argument pursuant to the rule that waivable affirmative defenses (of which preclusion is one) cannot be considered in determining the true amount in controversy. Thus, answers B and D are incorrect. Accordingly, the court would have subject matter jurisdiction in this case since the parties are diverse and the amount in controversy requirement has been met. Answer A is incorrect because diversity without the proper amount in controversy is not enough for §1332 jurisdiction.

38. Issue: Jurisdictional amount in controversy

The correct answer is **B**. This plaintiff is seeking judicial review of an arbitration agreement. Subject matter jurisdiction is predicated on §1332. And although the parties are diverse, the issue here is whether the "amount in controversy" exceeds $75,000. The circuit courts have upheld a trial court's decision to dismiss such a complaint for failure to meet the jurisdictional amount in controversy requirement. The courts rule that the amount in controversy in a case brought to vacate an arbitration award is the amount awarded in the arbitration proceeding and not the sum sought in the underlying claim. Thus, answer A is incorrect. They prefer a bright line rule to one that would predicate jurisdiction on the possibility that victory might result in a new arbitration award that would exceed the jurisdictional requirement. The controversy before it, the courts reason, is the arbitration award itself. Consequently, it is appropriate, they conclude, to consider only the amount awarded in that arbitration decision.

The same result also would obtain under the general rule that the jurisdictional amount must exist at the time of filing, since an arbitration award becomes subject to judicial review only when it is rendered. Similarly, the rule that the amount in controversy must appear on the face of the well pleaded complaint that initiated the particular action also supports this conclusion. The complaint in cases like this, the courts explain, seeks to vacate an arbitration award and not to litigate the merits of the underlying claim. Consequently, it is the amount awarded by the arbitrator that governs. Answer C is incorrect because diversity of citizenship is not enough, the complaint must also meet the amount in controversy requirement. Answer D is incorrect because federal courts can exercise jurisdiction over state law claims if the requirements of §1332 are met.

39. Issue: Domestic relations case exception to diversity

The correct answer is **C**. Since the parties are not seeking legal damages, we need to examine how compliance with the jurisdictional amount in controversy requirement is assessed. But also, although the case presents a seemingly clear-cut example of alienage jurisdiction falling within the language of §1332(a)(2), the Supreme Court has historically recognized an exception to diversity and alienage jurisdiction in cases involving domestic relations matters. Thus, answer B is incorrect. Since, as will be explained, this traditional exception applies to child custody cases, the courts would find that jurisdiction does not exist. Consequently, the jurisdictional amount problem is irrelevant. Therefore, answers A and D are incorrect.

The text of neither Article III nor §1332 makes any reference to an exception for domestic relations cases. Nevertheless, since 1859, the Supreme Court has recognized that certain domestic relations cases should not lie within the federal court's adjudicatory authority. In *Barber v. Barber*, 21 How. 582, 16 L. Ed. 226 (1859), the majority first articulated, in dictum and without explanation (the dissenters suggested that the reason was that domestic relations cases traditionally had not been heard in either law or equity courts in England, but in the country's ecclesiastical tribunals), the notion that federal courts did not possess subject matter jurisdiction over claims for divorce or alimony under their diversity jurisdiction power. The case involved an action by a wife to enforce a divorce and alimony decree that had already been entered by a state court. Nevertheless, the dictum was heeded and the practice began. Nearly 140 years later, this tradition was acknowledged and circumscribed by the Court in *Ankenbrandt v. Richards*, 504 U.S. 689, 112 S. Ct. 2206, 119 L. Ed. 2d 468 (1992). *Ankenbrandt* involved a tort claim brought by the mother on behalf of her two daughters alleging that the father and his female companion had subjected the children to sexual and physical abuse. The action was filed in federal district court on the basis of diversity of citizenship. After noting that neither the Constitution nor the jurisdictional statute contained any express limitation on diversity jurisdiction for domestic relations cases, the Court acknowledged that this historic exception to diversity jurisdiction was not constitutionally mandated. Rather, it stated, the ruling in *Barber* was a statement of the Court's interpretation of the statutory grant of jurisdiction. It then mentioned its post-*Barber* ruling in *In re Burrus*, 136 U.S. 586, 10 S. Ct. 850, 34 L. Ed. 500 (1890), in which the Court expanded the exception to include decrees in child custody cases. These exceptions, the Court explained, were ground in sound policy judgments. Since domestic relations decrees frequently involve retention of jurisdiction and utilization of social workers to monitor compliance, the Court reasoned, it was more efficient to channel these cases to the state courts since they are more adept in two ways at performing these functions than federal courts. First, the Court declared, state courts enjoy a closer working relationship than federal courts do with the relevant state and local government agencies that handle the issues associated with divorce, alimony, and child custody cases. Additionally, state courts have developed an expertise over the past 150 years in handling the issues that arise in the granting of decrees in such cases. For these reasons, the Court concluded, it made sense to retain the traditional exception from diversity jurisdiction for domestic relations cases, but only within a subset of that category. This exception, the Court insisted, applied only to suits involving the issuance of divorce, alimony, or child custody decrees.

Had this not involved child custody, we would have to determine whether or not the jurisdictional amount requirement had been met. In cases seeking only equitable or declaratory relief, the cases instruct the courts to look to the value of the rights in question. This is typically measured from the plaintiff's vantage point in terms of the value of whatever it is seeking to obtain in the suit. The impact of this doctrine was significantly abated as Congress enacted a series of jurisdictional statutes covering specific types of subject matter or where the U.S. government is a party, without regard to the amount in controversy. See, e.g., §§1333 (admiralty and maritime); 1334 (bankruptcy); 1336 (cases arising under federal laws regulating commerce); 1338 (patents, copyrights, trademarks); 1345 (United States as plaintiff); 1346 (United States as defendant); 1343 (civil rights actions); 1347 (United States as joint tenant). The coup de grace, for federal question cases, came in 1980 with the elimination of the amount in controversy requirement in §1331.

40. Issue: Domestic relations case exception to diversity

The correct answer is **A**. Although the Supreme Court has historically recognized an exception to diversity and alienage jurisdiction in cases involving domestic relations matters, the instant case is a tort claim for damages that does not involve the status of the domestic relations between the parties, such as a child custody or divorce proceeding. Therefore, the exception for domestic relations cases does not apply and the mother could invoke diversity jurisdiction. Thus, answer B is incorrect. The fact that the defendant is a citizen of the forum state is totally irrelevant to this problem. Therefore, answers C and D are incorrect.

41. Issue: Supplemental jurisdiction — pendent claim

The correct answer is **B**. A federal court must have subject matter jurisdiction over every claim in the lawsuit. The federal claim clearly falls within the court's

§1331 jurisdiction. The second claim, however, is a nondiverse state law claim since both parties are citizens of Indiana. Thus, it does not fall within the court's original jurisdiction under either §1331 or §1332. This, then, raises the question of whether the claim falls within the court's supplemental jurisdiction as provided by 28 U.S.C. §1367.

This is a situation that used to fall under the rubric of "pendent claim jurisdiction" first articulated by the Supreme Court in *UMW v. Gibbs*. It consists of a federal question claim and a nondiverse state claim brought by one plaintiff against one defendant. Congress codified this doctrine in §1367(a), which gives federal courts the discretion to exercise supplemental jurisdiction under these circumstances as long as the two claims form part of the same "case" under Article III of the Constitution, i.e., they arise out of a common nucleus of operative fact. If they do not, then the state claim must be dismissed and the federal court retains jurisdiction over the federal claim. If they do form part of the same "case," then the court has the discretion to exercise jurisdiction over the (nondiverse state law) claim that did not fall within its original jurisdiction. And §1367(c) lists the factors that the court should consider in deciding whether or not to decline to exercise this supplemental jurisdiction over the nondiverse state law claim.

In this hypothetical, both claims arise out of the same series of alleged acts of harassment and so the common nucleus test is satisfied. And none of the factors listed in §1367(c) such as predominance of state issues or novelty of state law issues or dismissal of the federal claim is present to justify dismissal of the state law claim. Therefore, the fact that there is no independent subject matter jurisdiction over the nondiverse state law claim is not fatal and so answer A is incorrect. Answer C is incorrect because the fact that the defendant is a forum citizen is irrelevant to this question. Answer D is incorrect because the fact that federal courts have concurrent, rather than exclusive subject matter jurisdiction over most federal claims is also irrelevant to this question.

42. Issue: Supplemental jurisdiction — pendent claim

The correct answer is **D**. The federal claim falls within the court's §1331 jurisdiction. The nondiverse state claim is subject to supplemental jurisdiction under §1367 if the two claims form part of the same case, i.e., arise out of a common nucleus of operative fact AND if none of the factors listed in §1367(c) justify declining to exercise such supplemental jurisdiction. Here, the two claims do form part of the same case but since the damages issue under state law is a question of first impression, this falls within the §1367(c)(1) factor justifying a decision to decline to exercise supplemental jurisdiction over the state claim. Answer A is incorrect because it fails to consider the discretionary factors of §1367(c). Answer B is incorrect because the fact that the parties are nondiverse is only fatal to jurisdiction under §1332, not under §1367. Answer C is incorrect because whether or not claims are nearly identical is not a standard for the exercise of supplemental jurisdiction.

43. Issue: Supplemental jurisdiction — pendent claim

The correct answer is **C**. The federal claim falls within the court's §1331 jurisdiction. The nondiverse state claim (both parties are citizens of Massachusetts) is subject to supplemental jurisdiction under §1367 only if the two claims form part of the same case, i.e., arise out of a common nucleus of operative fact and if none of the factors listed in §1367(c) justify declining to exercise such supplemental jurisdiction. Here, the facts giving rise to the price-fixing conspiracy are different from and unrelated to the facts giving rise to the breach of contract claim; the two claims do not form part of the same case. Therefore, there can be no supplemental jurisdiction over the nondiverse state law claim. Answer A is incorrect because the fact that the claim is a nondiverse state law claim would not preclude the exercise of supplemental jurisdiction if the requirements of §1367 were satisfied. Answer B is incorrect because it does not take into account the fact that two claims do not form part of the same case. Answer D is incorrect because the fact that the state law claim meets the jurisdictional amount in controversy requirement is not sufficient for §1332-based jurisdiction since the parties are not diverse.

44. Issue: Aggregation of value of diversity claims

The correct answer is **C**. This is a trick question. The adverse parties are of diverse citizenship. There clearly is §1332-based jurisdiction over the $100,000 claim since it meets both the diversity and amount in controversy requirements of §1332(a)(1). The second claim is for less than $75,000. But this does not make it a nondiverse state law claim that needs supplemental jurisdiction under §1367. The rules of aggregation permit a plaintiff to aggregate the value of multiple claims against a single defendant to meet the amount in controversy requirement of §1332. Therefore, since the value of these two claims can be aggregated, they both fit under the court's diversity jurisdiction. Any discussion of supplemental jurisdiction is irrelevant. Thus, answers A and B are incorrect. Answer D is incorrect because this fact is irrelevant to this question.

45. Issue: Supplemental jurisdiction — pendent parties

The correct answer is **A**. Prior to the enactment of §1367, the courts did not permit the exercise of pendent party jurisdiction, i.e., jurisdiction over a case with a claim against one defendant that fell within its original jurisdiction and a claim against a separate defendant that did not fall within its original jurisdiction. Congress changed that result, in part, with the enactment of §1367. Under §1367(a) if the plaintiff asserts a federal question claim against one defendant, the court can exercise supplemental jurisdiction over a nondiverse state law claim against a separate defendant if the two claims form part of the same case, i.e., arise out of a common nucleus of operative fact and if none of the factors listed in §1367(c) justify declining to exercise such supplemental jurisdiction. Here, the patent claim against the corporation is a federal question claim. The tort claim against the president does form part of the same case as that federal question claim since the infringing conduct gave rise to both claims. And none of the discretionary factors listed in §1367(c) justifies declining to exercise supplemental jurisdiction. Thus, jurisdiction can be exercised under §1367(a). Answer B is incorrect because §1367(a) does permit pendent party jurisdiction in cases involving a federal question claim. Answer C is incorrect because it is irrelevant and wrong as a matter of law. First of all, there is no aggregation of claims by a single plaintiff against multiple defendants. More important, the plaintiff and defendant Jones are not diverse and so §1332, and therefore its amount in controversy requirement, is inapplicable to this question. Answer D is wrong because §1331 has no amount in controversy requirement.

46. Issue: Supplemental jurisdiction — pendent parties

The correct answer is **D**. Prior to the enactment of §1367, the courts did not permit the exercise of pendent party jurisdiction, i.e., jurisdiction over a case with a claim against one defendant that fell within its original jurisdiction and a claim against a separate defendant that did not fall within its original jurisdiction. Congress changed that result, in part, with the enactment of §1367. Under §1367(a) if the plaintiff asserts a federal question claim against one defendant, the court can exercise supplemental jurisdiction over a nondiverse state law claim against a separate defendant if the two claims form part of the same case, i.e., arise out of a common nucleus of operative fact and if none of the factors listed in §1367(c) justify declining to exercise such supplemental jurisdiction. Here, the patent claim against the corporation is a federal question claim. The tort claim against the president, however, does not form part of the same case as the patent claim since it is based on acts of sexual harassment and the former claim arose out of the company's acts of infringement. Thus, supplemental jurisdiction under §1367(a) is not available, which makes answer A incorrect. Answer B is incorrect because §1367(a) does permit pendent party jurisdiction in cases involving a federal question claim. Answer C is incorrect because it is irrelevant and wrong as a matter of law. The plaintiff and defendant Jones are not diverse and so §1332, and therefore its amount in controversy requirement, is irrelevant to this question. Moreover, a plaintiff is not permitted to aggregate the value of claims against multiple defendants in a diversity-based case.

47. Issue: Supplemental jurisdiction — pendent party

The correct answer is **B**. The presence of one nondiverse plaintiff destroys the complete diversity required by §1332. Thus, under the contamination theory acknowledged by the Supreme Court in *Exxon Mobil*, the lack of diversity between Paul and Luther contaminates the diversity between Vernon and Luther and precludes the use of diversity jurisdiction as the basis for exercising original jurisdiction over any claim in the case. Thus, the court must dismiss both claims. With no original jurisdiction over either claim, there is no claim upon which to anchor any consideration of the exercise of supplemental jurisdiction. So even though the claim by Vernon against Luther would have met the requirements of §1332 had it been brought by itself, the contamination theory prevents it from falling within the court's original jurisdiction and thus cannot serve as the anchor for exercising supplemental jurisdiction over the claim by Paul against the nondiverse defendant Luther. Thus, answer A is incorrect. The fact that both claims exceed the amount in controversy requirement is irrelevant since Paul and Luther are not diverse and so answer C is incorrect. The fact that the action was filed in Texas is irrelevant to this problem and so answer D is incorrect.

48. Issue: Supplemental jurisdiction — pendent claim

The correct answer is **C**. Paine and Summers both assert a securities claim against Summit that arises under federal law and fits within the court's §1331 jurisdiction. But the state law claim by these two plaintiffs against Summit does not fall within the court's original §1332 jurisdiction since the two plaintiffs are nondiverse from the defendant; all are citizens of New York. The fact that Summit is also a citizen of Delaware (its state of incorporation) is irrelevant. Per §1332(c), since Summit's principal place of business is in New York, it is a citizen of New York and, therefore, there is no diversity of citizenship between it and the two plaintiffs. But, these claims are eligible, however, for supplemental jurisdiction under §1367(a) since they form part of the same case as the plaintiffs' §1331 claim as both the state and federal claims arise out of the same nucleus of operative fact — including material misrepresentations in a stock prospectus. And there is no suggestion that any of the factors listed in §1367(c) are present to justify declining to exercise supplemental jurisdiction. Answer A is incorrect because the state law claims do not fall within §1331 jurisdiction. Answer B is incorrect because the corporate law (state law) claims fall within §1367 jurisdiction. Answer D is incorrect because the absence of diversity is not jurisdictionally fatal since supplemental jurisdiction could be available if its requirements are met.

49. Issue: Supplemental jurisdiction — pendent party

The correct answer is **A**. Citizenship of a partnership consists of the citizenship of each and every partner. The plaintiffs' state law claims against Holcomb are nondiverse state law claims since all parties are citizens of New York as all of the defendant partnership's partners are citizens of New York. But the plaintiffs also assert a federal question claim against Summit and so the question is whether the court can exercise supplemental jurisdiction over the claims against Holcomb Brothers, i.e., whether the court can exercise what used to be called pendent party jurisdiction. Under §1367(a), pendent party jurisdiction can be exercised if the claim without its own independent basis of original jurisdiction is part of the same case as a claim falling under the court's §1331 jurisdiction. The plaintiffs assert a securities act (federal law) claim against Summit arising out of the misrepresentations in the prospectus. Thus, §1367(a) is in play and the exception in §1367(b) is inapposite. The pendent claim against the partnership arises out of the same nucleus of operative fact — the misrepresentations in the prospectus — as the federal claim against Summit. Thus, the basic requirement of §1367(a) is met. And none of the discretionary factors listed in §1367(c) that would justify declining to exercise supplemental jurisdiction appear to be present. This means that the court can exercise supplemental jurisdiction over these state law claims under §1367 and over the federal claims under §1331. Answer B is incorrect because the fact that the adverse parties to the corporate law claims are not diverse is not jurisdictionally fatal. Answer C is incorrect because the fact that the claim meets the amount in controversy requirement is not sufficient when the parties are not diverse. Answer D is incorrect because this is an irrelevant fact.

50. Issue: Supplemental jurisdiction — cross-claims

The correct answer is **D**. This claim is a cross-claim brought by one defendant against a co-defendant. It is a state law claim brought by one New York citizen against another New York citizen. Therefore there is no original jurisdiction over this claim under either §1331 or §1332. Under §1367(a), supplemental jurisdiction is available as to any claim that involves the joinder of additional parties, including cross-claims. Thus, the issue is whether the cross-claim forms part of the same case as the claim that falls within the court's original jurisdiction, i.e., the plaintiffs' federal securities claims against Summit. The answer to this is clearly no. That federal claim arose out of the creation of a prospectus containing misrepresentations. This breach of contract claim arises out of Summit's failure to pay the brokerage firm a royalty from the amount of Summit shares that the firm sold to the public. These two claims do not arise out of a common nucleus of operative fact and, therefore, supplemental jurisdiction over this claim is unavailable. Thus, answer C is incorrect. Answer A is incorrect because the claim is a nondiverse state law claim and so the fact that the claim meets the amount in controversy requirement is irrelevant. Answer B is incorrect because the absence of diversity is not jurisdictionally fatal since the claim falls within the court's supplemental jurisdiction under §1367(a).

51. Issue: Supplemental jurisdiction — third-party claims

The correct answer is **B**. This claim is a third-party claim for indemnity (often referred to as an impleader). It arises under state law and the adverse parties are both citizens of New York. Thus, there is no original jurisdiction over the claim under either §1331 or §1332. Under §1367(a), supplemental jurisdiction is available as to any claim that involves the joinder of additional parties, including third-party claims. Thus, the issue is whether the third-party claim for indemnity forms part of the same case as the claim that falls within the court's original jurisdiction, i.e., the plaintiffs' federal securities claims against Summit. The answer to this is clearly yes because that is precisely what a request for indemnity is — a request for reimbursement of any liability incurred by the indemnity plaintiff as a result of some claim filed by someone else against it. Thus, the "same case" requirement of §1367(a) is met since the indemnity is for liability incurred in connection with the federal securities claim asserted against it by Paine and Summers. And none of the discretionary factors listed in §1367(c) that would justify declining to exercise supplemental jurisdiction appear to be present. Thus, since supplemental jurisdiction is available, answer A is incorrect because the fact that the claim is a nondiverse state law claim is not jurisdictionally fatal. Answer C is incorrect because the indemnity claim does form part of the same case as the plaintiff's federal claim against Summit. Answer D is incorrect because this fact is irrelevant since jurisdiction over this claim is not and cannot be predicated upon §1332 since the adverse parties to this claim are not diverse.

52. Issue: Supplemental jurisdiction — counterclaims

The correct answer is **D**. This claim is a counterclaim. It arises under state law and the adverse parties are both citizens of New York. Thus, there is no original jurisdiction under either §1331 or §1332. But under §1367(a), supplemental jurisdiction is available over "all other claims" that form part of the "same case" as a claim that falls within that court's original jurisdiction. Thus, the issue is whether this counterclaim forms part of the same case as the plaintiff's claim that falls within the court's original jurisdiction, i.e., the plaintiffs' federal securities claims against Summit. The answer to this is clearly yes since it was the bringing of this securities claim that led to the malicious prosecution counterclaim. And none of the discretionary factors listed in §1367(c) that would justify declining to exercise supplemental jurisdiction appear to be present. Thus, since supplemental jurisdiction is available, answer A is incorrect because the fact that the claim is a nondiverse state law claim is not jurisdictionally fatal. Answer B is incorrect because this fact is irrelevant since jurisdiction over this nondiverse state law claim is not and cannot be predicated upon §1332. Answer C is not correct because the two claims do form part of the same case.

53. Issue: Supplemental jurisdiction — pendent party

The correct answer is **A**. The plaintiff's claim against the Missouri defendant falls within the court's §1332 jurisdiction because the diversity and amount in controversy requirements are met. But the plaintiff and the other defendant are both citizens of Rhode Island and since this is a state law claim, original jurisdiction is unavailable over this claim under either §1331 or §1332. Under the contamination rule acknowledged by the Supreme Court in *Exxon Mobil*, the presence of this nondiverse defendant contaminates the existence of diversity throughout the lawsuit and, therefore, no claim by a plaintiff can fall within the court's original jurisdiction under §1332. Thus, even though the plaintiff and the Missouri defendant are diverse, there can be no §1332-based original jurisdiction over this claim. Thus, both claims must be dismissed. Moreover, since there can be no original jurisdiction over the claim against the Missouri defendant, that claim cannot be used as the anchor for asserting supplemental jurisdiction over the state law claim against the nondiverse Rhode Island defendant. Thus, answer C is incorrect. Answer B is incorrect because this fact is irrelevant since §1367 cannot apply to this case. Answer D is incorrect because this fact is irrelevant since the parties to this claim are not diverse and therefore §1332 is inapposite.

54. Issue: Supplemental jurisdiction — counterclaims

The correct answer is **B**. Under the contamination rule acknowledged by the Supreme Court in *Exxon Mobil*, the presence of this nondiverse defendant contaminates the existence of diversity throughout the lawsuit and, therefore, no claim by a plaintiff can fall within the court's original jurisdiction under §1332. Thus, even though the plaintiff and the Missouri defendant are diverse, there can be no §1332-based original jurisdiction over the plaintiff's claim against that defendant. Thus, there is no original jurisdiction over the plaintiff's claims against either defendant and, therefore, both claims must be dismissed. Consequently, since there can be no original jurisdiction over the claim against either defendant, there is no claim that can serve as the basis or anchor for asserting supplemental jurisdiction over this counterclaim. Thus, answer A is incorrect. Answer C is incorrect because it is irrelevant. Answer D is incorrect because it is irrelevant as there is no possibility of exercising supplemental jurisdiction over any claim to this case.

55. Issue: Supplemental jurisdiction — third-party claims

The correct answer is **C**. This is a third-party complaint arising under state law between diverse parties but in which the amount in controversy is not in excess of $75,000. Therefore, there is no original jurisdiction over this claim under either §1331 or §1332. The question is whether there is supplemental jurisdiction over it. Under the contamination rule acknowledged by the Supreme Court in *Exxon Mobil*, the presence of the nondiverse Rhode Island defendant contaminated the existence of diversity throughout the lawsuit and, therefore, no claim by the plaintiff can fall within the court's original jurisdiction under §1332. Thus, even though the plaintiff and the Missouri defendant are diverse, there can be no §1332-based original jurisdiction over the plaintiff's claim against that defendant. Thus, there is no original jurisdiction over the plaintiff's claims against either defendant and, therefore, both claims must be dismissed. Consequently, since there is no original jurisdiction over the claim against either defendant, there is no claim that can serve as the basis or anchor for asserting supplemental jurisdiction over this third-party claim. Consequently, answer B is incorrect. Answer A is incorrect because it is not sufficient for the adverse parties to be diverse — the claim must also meet the amount in controversy requirement, which this $60,000 claim does not. Answer D is incorrect because it is irrelevant since supplemental jurisdiction is unavailable.

56. Issue: Supplemental jurisdiction — cross-claims

The correct answer is **D**. This is a cross-claim between diverse parties but which does not satisfy the jurisdictional amount in controversy requirement of §1332. Thus, no original jurisdiction exists under either §1332 or §1331. Does it fall within the court's supplemental jurisdiction? Under the contamination theory of *Exxon Mobil*, the presence of a nondiverse defendant contaminated the diversity between the plaintiff and the diverse defendant and eliminated §1332 as a basis for original jurisdiction over any of the plaintiff's claims. Consequently, there is no claim with original jurisdiction that can operate as the foundation for the exercise of supplemental jurisdiction over this claim. Thus, answer C is incorrect. Answer B is incorrect because §1367(b) is irrelevant here since there is no claim by plaintiff that falls within the court's §1332-based original jurisdiction as a result of the presence of a nondiverse defendant. Answer A is incorrect because the fact that the parties are diverse is not sufficient since this state law claim does not meet the amount in controversy requirement.

57. Issue: Time of filing rule

The correct answer is **B**. In *Grupo Dataflux v. Atlas*, the Supreme Court reaffirmed the time of filing rule, which states that in determining the existence of diversity of citizenship, one evaluates the citizenship of the parties at the time the complaint was filed. The defendant is a union and the established doctrine, including cases like *UMW v. Gibbs*, is that a union, like a partnership, is deemed to be a citizen of each and every state of which each of its members is a citizen. Thus, at the time of filing, the plaintiff was a citizen of Delaware and West Virginia and the defendant was a citizen of Pennsylvania and West Virginia. Thus, at that time, the parties were not diverse. In *Grupo Dataflux*, the Supreme Court refused to recognize an exception to the time of filing rule under circumstances exactly like those presented in this problem. It is true that an exception to the time of filing rule is recognized when the jurisdictional defect is cured by the dismissal of a party that had destroyed diversity. But that exception does not apply here, the Court in *Grupo* explained, because the union (there, a partnership) remained the party plaintiff. The loss of some of its members only changed its composition, it did not result in its dismissal as a party defendant. Thus, answer C is incorrect. Answer A is wrong because objections to subject matter jurisdiction are never waived. Answer D is incorrect because this fact is irrelevant to this problem.

58. Issue: Time of filing rule

The correct answer is **C**. It is established doctrine that the determination of the existence of diversity of citizenship is assessed at the time the complaint was filed. Under this time of filing rule, the parties were not diverse. But the courts also recognize an exception to the time of filing rule if the defect in complete diversity is cured by the dismissal of the party that destroyed diversity. Accordingly, since the nondiverse defendant was dismissed, the court would deny the motion to dismiss and rule that the dismissal rendered the case within the coverage of §1332(a)(1). Answer A is incorrect because objections to subject matter jurisdiction are never waived. Answer B is wrong because of this limited exception to the time of filing rule. Answer D is incorrect because this fact is irrelevant to this problem.

59. Issue: Tolling of limitations period in supplemental jurisdiction cases

The correct answer is **B**. To provide some protection to plaintiffs when an attempt to bring a nondiverse state law claim within the federal court's supplemental jurisdiction is unsuccessful, Congress enacted 28 U.S.C.

§1367(d). This statute provides that where a supplemental claim is dismissed, any state limitations period governing that dismissed claim is tolled for 30 days after the dismissal of the supplemental claim, unless state law provides for a longer tolling period. This means, in effect, that even if the state limitations period has expired by the time or shortly after the supplemental claim was dismissed, the plaintiff has 30 days to refile in state court without being subjected to the application of the state limitations period. But since this plaintiff waited more than 30 days to refile in state court, the tolling period has expired and thus the claim is subject to the terms of the state limitations period and must be dismissed. Thus, answer C is incorrect. Answer D is incorrect because this fact is irrelevant to this problem. Answer A is incorrect because the issue is whether the state claim was timely filed in state, not federal court.

60. Issue: Tolling of limitations period in supplemental jurisdiction cases

The correct answer is **A**. To provide some protection to plaintiffs when an attempt to bring a nondiverse state law claim within the federal court's supplemental jurisdiction is unsuccessful, Congress enacted 28 U.S.C. §1367(d). This statute provides that where a supplemental claim is dismissed, any state limitations period governing that dismissed claim is tolled for 30 days after the dismissal of the supplemental claim, unless state law provides for a longer tolling period. This means, in effect, that even if the state limitations period has expired by the time or shortly after the supplemental claim was dismissed, the plaintiff has 30 days to refile in state court without being subjected to the application of the state limitations period. The application of this provision would ordinarily mean, therefore, that since the plaintiff refiled his dismissed supplemental claim (it was supplemental because the parties are nondiverse and it was a state law claim and it was dismissed because it did not form part of the same case as the federal question claim) within 30 days of its dismissal, the state limitations period is tolled and the case should not be dismissed.

However, in *Raygor v. Regents of Univ. of Minnesota*, the Supreme Court construed §1367(d) not to apply when a supplemental claim is a state law claim against a nonconsenting state that was dismissed on Eleventh Amendment grounds. Accordingly, answer B is incorrect. For §1367(d) to be construed to apply in this situation, the court ruled in *Raygor*, its intention to abrogate the constitutional impediment to federal jurisdiction would have to have been manifested in unmistakably clear language. Since §1367(d) did not contain a clear statement of any intent to abrogate sovereign immunity, the Court reasoned, it should not be read to authorize the exercise of supplemental jurisdiction over a state law claim against a nonconsenting state defendant. Therefore, it held that the state law claims were properly dismissed pursuant to the terms of the governing state limitations provision. Answer C is incorrect because while it is crucial that the claim was dismissed on sovereign immunity grounds, the mere fact that the defendant was a state was not the basis for the decision since it relates only to state law claims against nonconsenting states. Answer D is an incorrect statement of law.

61. Issue: Well pleaded complaint rule

The correct answer is **D**. Under §1441(a), a case is removable by the defendant if it falls within the court's original jurisdiction. Since the parties here are not diverse, the only possible basis of original jurisdiction is §1331, i.e., the federal question provision. But under the well pleaded complaint rule, a federal question must appear within a well pleaded complaint, i.e., be an element of the plaintiff's prima facie case and not appear only in the defendant's answer or in the plaintiff's complaint in the form of a reply to an anticipated defense. Here, the constitutional question contained within the plaintiff's complaint is not a part of her well pleaded complaint. Rather, it is only a reply to an anticipated defense. Thus, the claim is not removable and answer A is incorrect. Answer B is simply an incorrect statement of law. Answer C is wrong because the parties are not diverse and so §1332 is unavailable as a basis for removal.

62. Issue: Master of the complaint rule

The correct answer is **C**. Since this is a nondiverse state law claim, the only possible basis for removing the case under §1441(a) is the presence of a federal question claim. But under the master of the complaint rule, the plaintiff can choose which claims she wishes to assert as long as federal law has not preempted the field that governs this claim. Here, federal law does not preempt the existence of state antidiscrimination law and so the master of the complaint rule applies. Thus, answer B is incorrect. Answer A is incorrect because the absence of diversity is not what prohibits removal here because the claim also does not meet the amount in controversy requirement, which would eliminate the possibility of a diversity-based removal even if the parties had been citizens of different states. Answer D is incorrect because the defendant is not a citizen of the forum state since the suit was filed in New Mexico.

63. Issue: Jurisdictional amount in controversy

The correct answer is **D**. The parties are diverse and the claim arises solely under state law. Thus, answer B is incorrect. The issue here is whether the plaintiff's claim meets the amount in controversy requirement. The damages claim does not since it is not in excess of $75,000. But there is also a request for equitable relief in the form of an injunction. In determining whether claims for equitable relief meet the amount in controversy requirement, the court attempts to place some monetary value on the right asserted by the plaintiff from the plaintiff's perspective. Since a single plaintiff can aggregate the value of multiple claims against a single defendant to meet the amount in controversy requirement, the value of that right would only have to be one penny to meet the statutory requirement. Surely the asserted right is worth at least one cent. Thus, answer A is incorrect. Answer C is factually incorrect — the defendant is not a citizen of California, the forum state.

64. Issue: Removal by a forum defendant

The correct answer is **B**. The parties are diverse and the claim meets the jurisdictional amount requirement. Thus, the claim falls within the federal court's original jurisdiction under §1332. But there is an exception to the general removal rule. Section 1441(b) provides that a diversity case cannot be removed by a defendant who is a citizen of the forum state. Thus, answers A and C are incorrect. Answer D is incorrect because this fact is irrelevant to removal.

65. Issue: Removal by a forum defendant

The correct answer is **C**. While it is true that the defendant is a citizen of the forum state, the exception in §1441(b) barring removal by a defendant who is a citizen of the forum state only applies to diversity-based removals. Here, the basis of removal is §1331 because the plaintiff asserted a federal statutory claim. Thus, §1441(b) is inapposite and the claim is removable. Therefore, answer B is incorrect. Answer A is incorrect because the fact that the parties are diverse is irrelevant. Section 1441(b) does not apply when the court has original jurisdiction founded on a federal law claim, regardless of whether the parties also happen to be of diverse citizenship. Answer D is incorrect because this fact is irrelevant to removal.

66. Issue: Time of filing rule

The correct answer is **D**. As applied to removed cases, the time of filing rule means that if removal is based on diversity of citizenship, the parties must be diverse BOTH at the time the state court complaint was filed and at the time of removal. This is a state law claim and so answer A is incorrect. Although the parties were diverse at the time the complaint was filed, since the defendant had changed his domicile before removing the case, the parties were no longer diverse at the time of removal. Thus, removal could not be based on §1332 and so answer B is incorrect. Since the case did not fall within the federal court's original jurisdiction, it was not removable under §1441(a). Therefore, we never get to §1441(b) and so the fact that the defendant was a forum citizen at the time of removal does not matter. Thus, answer C is incorrect.

67. Issue: Time of filing rule

The correct answer is **C**. When the defendant removed the case, the claim was removable because it met both the diversity and amount in controversy requirements of §1332. But the plaintiff did not want to be in federal court and so, after removal, she amended the complaint to state a claim that did not meet the amount in controversy ("in excess of" $75,000) requirement of §1332. The Supreme Court has held, in *St. Paul Mercury Indemnity*, that removability is gauged by the pleadings at time of the filing of the notice of removal and not thereafter. Thus, answer B is incorrect and the plaintiff's attempt to defeat federal jurisdiction by amending her complaint after the case was removed will be unavailing and the court will deny the motion to remand. Answer A is incorrect because this fact is irrelevant to this problem. Answer D is incorrect because this fact is irrelevant to this problem.

68. Issue: Removal by multiple defendants

The correct answer is **A**. Under §1441(a), a case involving multiple defendants is removable only if the claims against each defendant fall within the court's original jurisdiction. Here the claim against the boss does meet the requirements of §1331 (there is no amount in controversy requirement for federal question claims). But the local grocery store defendant presumably is a citizen of the state in which it is located, which makes it nondiverse from the plaintiff. Therefore, the suit is not removable under §1332 because these parties are not diverse. The only way to avoid that result would be to conclude that the joinder of the grocery store was collusive, i.e., for the purpose of defeating diversity and, therefore, under §1359, the citizenship of this party could be ignored for jurisdictional purposes. But proving collusive joinder is a heavy burden to sustain. The defendant must convince the court to a legal certainty that the plaintiff could not recover anything against the allegedly fraudulently joined defendant. There are no facts here to suggest such a result. Consequently, the case is not removable because of the lack of diversity. Answer B is incorrect because this fact is irrelevant to this problem. Answer C is incorrect because this party is not diverse from the plaintiff so the fact that the amount in controversy requirement has been met is irrelevant. Answer D is incorrect because §1441(b) does not come into play unless the case is otherwise removable under §1441(a) and the fact that this party is nondiverse from the plaintiff makes it nonremovable under §1441(a) and so §1441(b) is inapposite.

69. Issue: Removal under changed circumstances

The correct answer is **A**. Here, the question is whether an initially nonremovable case (because of lack of complete diversity) can "become" removable because of some change in the status quo. Specifically, the plaintiff voluntarily dismissed a state law claim against a nondiverse defendant, thereby creating complete diversity between the plaintiff and the remaining defendant. Where the plaintiff effectuates the change in the status quo, the case is removable. Section 1446(b) directly addresses this scenario by providing that where the case stated by the original complaint is not removable, but a change is made thereafter that renders the case removable, the defendant is not precluded by the generally applicable requirement in §1446(a) that the notice of removal be filed within 30 days after receipt of the initial complaint. Rather, §1446(b) provides the defendant with the answer of filing a notice of removal within 30 days of receipt of an amended pleading or a motion or other paper from which the defendant can determine that the case has "become" removable. Here, the defendant removed the case one day after the change and so removal is proper and so answer B is incorrect. Answer C is incorrect because this fact is irrelevant. Answer D is irrelevant because the defendant as to that claim has been dismissed and is now irrelevant to the question of removal.

This extended time frame for removal because of changed circumstances, however, is limited in diversity-based removal. In diversity cases that were not removable on the basis of the initial pleading, §1446(b) provides for a one-year statute of limitations on removal dating from the commencement of the suit.

But since the plaintiff's dismissal occurred less than one year after the original complaint was filed, this time limit is inapposite.

70. Issue: Removal under changed circumstances

The correct answer is **D**. Here, the question is whether an initially nonremovable case (because of lack of complete diversity) can "become" removable because of some change in the status quo. Specifically, the plaintiff voluntarily dismissed a state law claim against a nondiverse defendant, thereby creating complete diversity between the plaintiff and the remaining defendant.

Where the plaintiff effectuates the change in the status quo, the case is removable. Section 1446(b) directly addresses this scenario by providing that where the case stated by the original complaint is not removable, but a change is made thereafter that renders the case removable, the defendant is not precluded by the generally applicable requirement in §1446(a) that the notice of removal be filed within 30 days after receipt of the initial complaint. Rather, §1446(b) provides the defendant with the answer of filing a notice of removal within 30 days of receipt of an amended pleading or a motion or other paper from which the defendant can determine that the case has "become" removable. Here, the defendant removed the case one day after the change and so removal would seem to be appropriate. However, this statutorily extended time frame for removal because of changed circumstances is limited in diversity-based removal. In diversity cases, such as this one, that were not removable on the basis of the initial pleading, §1446(b) provides for a one-year statute of limitations on removal dating from the commencement of the suit. Here the case became removable when the nondiverse defendant was dismissed but that occurred two years after commencement of the litigation, thereby exceeding the time limit set forth in §1446(b). For that reason, the case is not removable and answer A is incorrect. Answer B is not correct because the remaining defendant is not a citizen of the forum state. Answer C is incorrect because this fact is irrelevant to this problem.

71. Issue: Removal under changed circumstances

The correct answer is **C**. Where the plaintiff effectuates the change in the status quo, the case is removable. Section 1446(b) directly addresses this scenario by providing that where the case stated by the original complaint is not removable, but a change is made thereafter that renders the case removable, the defendant is not precluded by the generally applicable requirement in §1446(a) that the notice of removal be filed within 30 days after receipt of the initial complaint. Rather, §1446(b) provides the defendant with the answer of filing a notice of removal within 30 days of receipt of an amended pleading or a motion or other paper from which the defendant can determine that the case has "become" removable. Here, however, the change in the status of the case's removability is occasioned by a court order as opposed to a voluntary act undertaken by the plaintiff. Under these circumstances, the majority of lower courts hold that the case is not removable. This decision is based on the theory that the court's action in dismissing the defendant might be reversed on appeal and then the case would ultimately be determined to be nonremovable and the federal district court would have wasted time and resources on the action. Therefore, the court will not consider the changed circumstances in determining the presence of complete diversity. So since there was not complete diversity here prior to the dismissal, the state law case is nonremovable. Answer A is incorrect because the remaining defendant is a citizen of Delaware and not a citizen of the forum state. Answer B is incorrect because there remains lack of complete diversity since the court will not disregard a defendant dismissed per court order. Answer D is incorrect because this fact is irrelevant to this problem.

72. Issue: Removal by plaintiff

The correct answer is **A**. Section 1441(a) provides for removal "by the defendant or the defendants." Here, the defendant could not remove the case because the plaintiff's claim is a nondiverse state law claim. But the defendant's counterclaim is a federal question claim under §1331. The question raised, then, is whether a case can be removed on the basis of a counterclaim that falls within the court's original jurisdiction. But this, in turn, really depends upon whether a "plaintiff" can be considered a "defendant" for §1441(a) purposes when that "plaintiff" is the responding party to the claim serving as the basis for removal (i.e., the counterclaim). The law is clear on this point. The Supreme Court, in *Shamrock Oil & Gas Corp. v. Sheets*, held that a plaintiff is not deemed a "defendant" for removal purposes even when it is the counter-defendant to a claim within the federal court's original jurisdiction. Thus, answer B is incorrect. Answer C is incorrect because that fact would only be relevant if the claim were removable on the basis of diversity and that is not the case here. Answer D is incorrect because this fact is irrelevant to this problem.

73. Issue: Removal by plaintiff

The correct answer is **A**. Section 1441(a) provides for removal "by the defendant or the defendants." Here, the removing party is the plaintiff who is the defendant to a cross-claim by a co-plaintiff. (The actual defendant could not remove the case because the plaintiff's claim is a nondiverse state law claim.) The question raised, then, is whether a case can be removed on the basis of a state law cross-claim that meets all requirements set forth in §1332 for original jurisdiction based on diversity of citizenship. But this in turn really depends upon whether a "plaintiff" can be considered a "defendant" for §1441(a) purposes when that "plaintiff" is the responding party to the claim (here a cross-claim) serving as the basis for removal. The law is clear on this point. The Supreme Court, in *Shamrock Oil & Gas Corp. v. Sheets*, held that a plaintiff is not deemed a "defendant" for removal purposes even when it is the counterdefendant to a claim within the federal court's original jurisdiction. The courts apply this same doctrine to bar removal on the basis of a diverse cross-claim asserted by one plaintiff against a co-plaintiff. Thus, answer B is incorrect. Answer C is incorrect because since the case cannot be removed on the basis of a diverse cross-claim against a plaintiff, the fact that the responding party to that diverse claim is a citizen of the forum state is irrelevant. Answer D is wrong because this fact is irrelevant to this problem.

74. Issue: Removal under §1441(c)

The correct answer is **B**. Under §1441(a), a case that contains both a removable and nonremovable claim can be removed if two conditions are met. First, the removable claim must be a federal question, and not a diverse state law claim. Second, the removable and nonremovable claims must be determined to be "separate and independent" from one another. If both of these requirements are met, the entire case is removable subject to the federal court's discretionary decision to remand all claims in which state law predominates. Here, the plaintiff did assert a §1331 federal question claim against the manufacturer. The claim against the printer is not separately removable because it does not meet either of the requirements of §1332 and is not a federal question claim. Since this otherwise nonremovable claim arises out of a totally different collection of facts from the federal claim and the resolution of that contract claim would have no bearing on the disposition of the federal claim, the two claims clearly are separate and independent. Finally, §1441(c) does provide the federal judge with the discretion to remand all claims in which state law predominates. This language has been interpreted to mean that the judge should look at the entire action, not just the nonremovable claim (which is typically a nondiverse state law claim) to determine whether the federal law claim is so minor or unimportant that state law can be said to predominate in the civil action taken as a whole. Here, there is no evidence that this is the case. Consequently, the entire case is removable under §1441(c). Answer A is incorrect because the fact that the claim against the retailer is a nondiverse claim is not fatal to removal in light of §1441(c). Answer C is incorrect for the same reason. Answer D is incorrect because the citizenship of a defendant to a federal question claim is irrelevant to removal and since the claim against the retailer is not independently removable under §1441(a), the exception to such removability provided in §1441(b) does not come into play.

75. Issue: Removal under §1441(c)

The correct answer is **B**. The claim against the New Jersey citizen is removable because it meets all the requirements for original jurisdiction under §1332. However, the other claim is a nondiverse state law claim and, therefore, separately nonremovable. Under §1441(a), a case that contains both a removable and nonremovable claim can be removed, but only if two conditions are met. First, the removable claim must be a federal question, and not a diverse state law claim. Second, the removable and nonremovable claims must be determined to be "separate and independent" from one another. If both of these requirements are met, the entire case is removable subject to the federal court's discretionary decision to remand all claims in which state law predominates. But here the removable claim is not a federal question claim, but a diversity claim. Therefore, removal under §1441(c) is unavailable and so it does not matter whether these two claims are separate and independent. Thus, answer A is incorrect. Answer C is incorrect because citizenship of a removing defendant is irrelevant as to a federal question claim and the claim against the New York defendant is nondiverse so §1441(b) is inapplicable. Answer D is incorrect because this fact is irrelevant to this problem.

76. Issue: Removal under §1441(c)

The correct answer is **A**. This problem involves a federal law claim against one defendant and a diverse state law claim against another defendant who is a citizen of the forum state. Although the state law claim against the Pennsylvania dredging company satisfies both the diversity and jurisdictional amount requirements of §1332(a), this defendant is a forum citizen and therefore is precluded from removing that claim under §1441(b). Consequently, §1441(a) cannot be used as the basis for removing the entire case since §1441(b) prohibits removal of the diversity claim against the forum defendant. But can the case then be analyzed as involving a §1331 claim and a separate and independent otherwise nonremovable claim and, therefore, be deemed removable under 1441(c)? This question turns upon the meaning of "otherwise non-removable" for §1441(c) purposes. If the fact that the diverse defendant is a forum citizen makes this claim (which satisfies all the requirements of §1332) "otherwise non-removable" for §1441(c) purposes, then the case will be removable if the two claims are separate and independent. Although the Supreme Court has not ruled on this question, the prevailing view is that a case is nonremovable for §1441(c) purposes *only* if it does not fall within the federal court's original jurisdiction. Since this diverse claim meets all the requirements of §1332, it does fall within the court's original jurisdiction. The bar to removability under §1441(a) is found not in §1332 but in §1441(b), i.e., the courts treat this as a "procedural" and not a "jurisdictional" obstacle to removal. Consequently, since this diversity claim against a forum defendant does fall within the court's "original" jurisdiction, it is *not* "otherwise non-removable" for §1441(c) purposes and, therefore, it cannot be removed under §1441(c). Therefore, answer B is incorrect. Answer C is incorrect because the citizenship of a defendant to a federal question claim is irrelevant to removal. Answer D is wrong because this fact is not relevant to this problem.

77. Issue: Derivative jurisdiction in removal

The correct answer is **B**. The problem here is that the defendant is seeking to remove a case from a state court that did not have subject matter jurisdiction over the case because it arose under a statute that fell within the federal courts' exclusive subject matter jurisdiction. Prior to 1985, the prevailing jurisprudence held that a case could not be properly removed from a state court that did not initially possess subject matter jurisdiction. Since the plaintiff's patent infringement action falls within the exclusive jurisdiction of the federal courts, the state court did not have subject matter jurisdiction of the removed case. The judicially created doctrine of "derivative jurisdiction" was eliminated when, as part of the Judicial Improvements Act of 1985, Congress added §1441(f) to the removal statute. Under this provision, therefore, the case is removable and answer A is incorrect. Answer C is incorrect because the citizenship of a defendant to a federal question claim is irrelevant to removal. Answer D is incorrect because the value of the matter in controversy is irrelevant to a federal question claim.

78. Issue: Waiver of personal jurisdiction objection

The correct answer is **B**. The prevailing rule is that removal does not operate to waive any defenses, including an objection to jurisdiction or sufficiency of service. The case is treated, for these purposes, as if it were originally brought in federal court. Thus, answer A is incorrect. Answer C is incorrect because that fact goes to subject matter, rather than personal jurisdiction. Answer D is incorrect because being a noncitizen is not, by itself, fatal to the exercise of personal jurisdiction if a noncitizen can constitutionally be subject to a state long-arm statute.

79. Issue: Precedence of subject matter over personal jurisdiction objection

The correct answer is **B**. The defendant has removed a state law claim between diverse parties that does not satisfy the amount in controversy requirement of §1332. Consequently, the federal district court does not have subject matter jurisdiction. Since objections to subject matter jurisdiction are not waivable and, in fact, can be raised by the court *sua sponte*, this problem raises the question of whether this court can adjudicate the personal jurisdiction challenge prior to determining the existence of subject matter jurisdiction. Obviously, resolution of the subject matter jurisdiction question in this instance pretermits consideration of the defendant's personal jurisdiction challenge and the case will be remanded to the state court since the claim is not removable since it does not meet the amount in controversy requirement of §1332. This, in turn, means that to the extent the defendant wants to adjudicate the personal jurisdiction issue, a state, rather than a federal, judge will resolve it. While that result might, in some cases, frustrate the defendant's desire to have a federal judge resolve that question, since many personal jurisdiction questions involve the construction of state long-arm statutes, this result promotes interests of federalism/comity by leaving the interpretation of state law to the state court. This was precisely the issue addressed by the Supreme Court in *Ruhrgas v. Marathon Oil Co.* Resolving a split among the circuits, and reversing an *en banc* decision by the Fifth Circuit, the Court tried to take all of the foregoing considerations into account. Speaking for a unanimous Court, Justice Ginsburg announced that "there is no unyielding jurisdictional hierarchy." Rather, the district court in a removed case should consider whether disposition of either the personal or subject matter jurisdiction issue would or would not involve a complex issue. In cases where the personal jurisdiction inquiry is either straightforward (as here) or turns primarily on a federal constitutional issue, the federal district court does not abuse its discretion by turning first to personal jurisdiction, particularly when the subject matter jurisdictional question is either complex or novel. Therefore, this court can consider the personal jurisdiction question even though it does not have subject matter jurisdiction over this claim. Therefore, answer C is incorrect. Answer A is incorrect because the prevailing rule is that removal does not operate to waive any defenses, including an objection to personal jurisdiction. Answer D is incorrect because being a noncitizen is not, by itself, fatal to the exercise of personal jurisdiction if a noncitizen can constitutionally be subject to a state long-arm statute.

80. Issue: Venue

The correct answer is **C**. Venue in diversity cases is governed by 28 U.S.C. §1391(a). Under §1391(a)(1) venue will lie in a federal judicial district in which any defendant resides as long as all defendants reside in the same state. Although the two defendants reside in different federal judicial districts (the Northern and Central Districts of California), they both reside in the State of California. Therefore, venue would lie in either the Central (Los Angeles) or Northern (San Francisco) District. Answer A is incorrect because the plaintiff's choice of venue is not dispositive. Answer B is incorrect because residence of the plaintiff is irrelevant for venue purposes. Answer D is incorrect because only one of the defendants needs to reside in the chosen district if both defendants reside in the same multi-district state.

81. Issue: Venue

The correct answer is **B**. Venue in diversity cases is governed by 28 U.S.C. §1391(a). The only answers under this statute are the district in which any defendant resides if they all reside in the same state, a district in which a substantial part of the events giving rise to the claim occurred, or a district in which any defendant is subject to personal jurisdiction if there is no other district in the United States that would qualify under either of the first two answers. None of the defendants resides in New York so defendant residence does not provide venue. The events giving rise to the claim occurred in California so that does not provide venue in New York. Even if the defendants would be subject to personal jurisdiction in New York, that is not a basis for venue because that fall-back answer is only available if there is no other district in the United States that would meet either of the prior two tests. Since venue would lie in any judicial district in California, we cannot rely on the fall-back provision and so answer C is incorrect. Therefore, venue does not lie in New York City. The fact that the plaintiff resides there is irrelevant because plaintiff's residence is irrelevant to a venue determination. Answer A is incorrect because the plaintiff's choice of venue is not dispositive. Answer D is incorrect because this proposition is irrelevant to this problem.

82. Issue: Venue

The correct answer is **A**. Venue in diversity cases is governed by 28 U.S.C. §1391(a). The only answers under this statute are the district in which any defendant resides if they all reside in the same state, a district in which a substantial part of the events giving rise to the claim occurred, or a district in which any defendant is subject to personal jurisdiction if there is no other district in the United States that would qualify under either of the first two answers. Neither of the defendants resides in the chosen district and the events giving rise to the claim did not occur within that district. Can we then rely on the personal jurisdiction-based fall-back position? Only if there is no other federal district in which venue would lie under either of the first two answers. Since there is no district in the United States in which both defendants reside and there is no district in the United States where the events giving rise to the claim occurred, then the fall-back provision comes into play. And this fall-back provision states that venue will lie in a district in which "any defendant" is subject to personal jurisdiction. But neither defendant is subject to personal jurisdiction in Pennsylvania so venue would not lie in any district in that state. Since Leroy is subject to personal jurisdiction in Michigan and Sally is subject to personal jurisdiction in Illinois, venue would lie in either the Eastern District of Michigan or the Northern District of Illinois. Therefore, answer B is incorrect. Answer C is incorrect because this factor is irrelevant to a venue determination. Answer D is incorrect because the plaintiff's residence is irrelevant to a venue determination.

83. Issue: Venue

The correct answer is **C**. This case involves two defendants — one natural person and one corporation. Since residence is the relevant concept for venue purposes, we need to know the definition of residence for a corporate defendant. Under the terms of §1391(c), a corporate defendant resides in any federal judicial district in which the corporation is subject to personal jurisdiction. And in multi-district states, the corporation is deemed to reside in any district in that state within which its contacts would be sufficient to subject it to personal jurisdiction if that district were considered to be a separate state. Here, defendant Sally is a resident of the Northern District of Illinois (Chicago). The defendant rental company clearly resides in Hawaii and is also subject to personal jurisdiction in the state under whose laws it is incorporated — Delaware. But it does not have any contact with Pennsylvania that would justify determining that it would be subject to personal jurisdiction in any part of Pennsylvania. Consequently, Bike Rentals does not reside in the Eastern District of Pennsylvania (Philadelphia). Therefore, we now have two defendants, each of whom resides in different states. Thus, residence of defendants is not useful for venue purposes. The events occurred in Hawaii so that will not support jurisdiction in the Eastern District of Pennsylvania (Philadelphia). And since the events occurred in Hawaii, venue would not lie in Philadelphia under §1391(a)(2). We cannot even consider the fall-back provision of (a)(3) since venue clearly would lie in Hawaii. Answer A is incorrect because the residence of the plaintiff is irrelevant under the federal venue statute. Answer B is incorrect because the company is not subject to personal jurisdiction in Pennsylvania. Answer D is incorrect because it is irrelevant.

84. Issue: Residence of alien for venue purposes

The correct answer is **A**. Subject matter jurisdiction is predicated on §1331(a)(1) (as to the claim against Sally) and §1331(a)(2) (as to the claim against Pedalo). So the governing venue statute is §1391(a), which provides for venue in the district where the defendant resides. Since Sally resides in Chicago, venue is clearly appropriate as to the claim against her. Pedalo is a foreign company. But §1391(d) expressly provides that an alien can be sued in any federal district. Thus, venue lies in Chicago as to both claims. Answer B is incorrect because aliens can be sued in any federal district. Answer C is incorrect because the residence of the plaintiff is irrelevant for venue purposes. Answer D is incorrect because the fact that the accident did not occur in the chosen venue does not preclude venue if venue can be predicated on the residence of the defendant(s).

85. Issue: Venue in removed case

The correct answer is **C**. This case was removed to federal court and was not initially filed there. The removal statute, §1441(a), contains its own special venue provision. It provides that removed cases can be removed only to the district court for the district in which the state court is located. The venue rules of §1391 do not apply to removed cases. Thus, the fact that none of the three subsections of §1391(a) would be satisfied in this case does not deprive the federal court in West Virginia from having venue over the action. Therefore, answers A and B are incorrect. Answer D is incorrect because the residence of the plaintiff is irrelevant for federal venue purposes.

86. Issue: Transfer of venue

The correct answer is **C**. In this problem, the defendant seeks to transfer the case to a district that would not have personal jurisdiction over him. This calls into question whether or not that district is one in which the case "might have been brought" by the plaintiff within the meaning of §1404. In its well-known, though controversial, ruling in *Hoffman v. Blaski*, the Supreme Court construed this language to mean that the transferor court must possess personal jurisdiction over the defendant and any lack of jurisdiction cannot be cured by the defendant's consent to the exercise of jurisdiction over it by the transferor court. The perennially raised objection to the ruling in *Hoffman* asserts that the Court's wooden interpretation of the "might have been brought" language of §1404 means that a case cannot be transferred to a district where, in fact, the action could be tried. Presumably, since the defendant is willing to consent to the exercise of jurisdiction for the purposes of effecting a transfer, it would have been willing to consent to the exercise of jurisdiction by that court if the plaintiff had initially chosen that forum. Supporters of the *Hoffman* doctrine, alternatively, insist that its bright line rule minimizes the variables that have to be evaluated in ruling on a §1404 motion by limiting the court to an evaluation of the complaint and avoiding an independent investigation of the defendants' willingness to waive objections to personal jurisdiction. Therefore, answer A is incorrect. Answer B is incorrect because this fact, if true, is irrelevant to this problem. Answer D is incorrect because this fact is irrelevant to this problem.

87. Issue: Transfer of venue

The correct answer is **B**. The crucial factor in this problem is that the transferor court in Houston does not have personal jurisdiction over the defendant. So we must determine whether this defect is fatal to the court's ability to transfer under either §1404. In *Goldlawr v. Heiman*, the Court ruled that a court in which venue was improperly laid could still transfer a case under §1406 even if it also lacked personal jurisdiction over the defendant. This broad construction of §1406 was warranted, the Court reasoned, in order to avoid the injustice of compelling the forfeiture of some or all of a plaintiff's claim simply because it had made an erroneous guess as to "the existence of some elusive fact of the kind upon which venue provisions often turn." The Court also stated that this result would promote the congressional objective of removing obstacles that might "impede an expeditious and orderly adjudication of cases and controversies." In the instant hypothetical, the transferor court does not have venue since the Nevada defendant does not reside in that Texas district and the facts giving rise to the claim did not occur in Texas, but in Nevada. Additionally, the facts indicate that the Nevada defendant would not be subject to the personal jurisdiction of the Texas court. But under *Goldlawr*, the Texas court can cure both of these defects by transferring the case under §1406 to a district in which it "could have been brought." Clearly, as both venue and personal jurisdiction would be available in the transferee court in Nevada, the interests of justice will be served by transferring the case there. Nevertheless, the defendant here sought to transfer the case to Nevada under §1404. He did not raise an issue as to whether venue was proper in Houston and then hope that the court would find that venue was improper and transfer the case under §1406. Nevertheless, to avoid unjust dismissals, the courts extend the rationale of *Goldlawr* to §1404-based transfers. Thus, since the action could have been brought by the plaintiff in Nevada since venue would lie there and the defendant is subject to personal jurisdiction there, the court should grant the motion. Answer A is wrong because the ruling in *Goldlawr* has been extended to make this fact non-fatal to a §1404-based transfer motion. Answer C is incorrect for the same reason. Answer D is wrong because the facts indicate that the motion was made under §1404, not under §1406.

88. Issue: Transfer of venue by plaintiffs

The correct answer is **B**. In *Van Dusen v. Barrack*, the Supreme Court held that when a case is transferred per §1404, transfer should have no impact on the substantive law to be applied to the case since the original court was an appropriate venue under the governing venue rules. Thus, the transferee court must apply the substantive law, including the choice of law rules, which the transferor court would have applied in the absence of a transfer. This problem raises the question of whether the plaintiff can take advantage of this doctrine by filing the action in the district that would apply the most advantageous law and then seeking to transfer the case to a more convenient district. The first question, therefore, is whether a plaintiff is ever allowed to transfer a case from the forum that it chose. The text of §1404 contains no defendant-specific language. And the courts uniformly have construed this language as not precluding plaintiffs from seeking a transfer. Thus, answer A is incorrect. But should this blatant forum shopping by a plaintiff be encouraged by allowing plaintiffs to seek a change of their own chosen venue? This issue was placed directly before the Supreme Court in *Ferens v. John Deere Co.*, where the Court rejected the defendant's call for an exception to the *Van Dusen* rule in plaintiff-initiated transfers under §1404. Instead, it held the transferee court must apply the law of the transferor forum regardless of which party filed the §1404 motion. Thus, answer C is incorrect. Thus, the only remaining question is whether Chicago, the transferee court, is a district in which the action might have been brought, i.e., was the defendant subject to personal jurisdiction there and does venue lie there. Clearly the answer to that is yes since the defendant resides there. Thus, the motion to transfer should be granted. Answer D is incorrect because it is irrelevant to this problem.

89. Issue: *Forum non conveniens*

The correct answer is **A**. The defendant here is relying on the doctrine of *forum non conveniens* as the basis for dismissing an action over which the court clearly has subject matter jurisdiction, in which venue lies, and with respect to a defendant over which it clearly has personal jurisdiction. Courts will grant this motion upon a showing not only that the chosen forum is extremely inconvenient but that a distinctly more convenient forum exists in which the court would have subject matter jurisdiction, venue, and personal jurisdiction. In the seminal case of *Piper Aircraft v. Reyno*, the Supreme Court indicated that, in determining whether an alternative forum exists, if the remedy provided by the alternative forum is so clearly inadequate or unsatisfactory that it is no remedy at all, the unfavorable change in law may be given substantial weight and the district court may conclude that dismissal would not be in the interests of justice. But the Court also stated that this standard is not met merely when the remedy provided by the alternate forum is either more difficult to obtain or not as lavish as that provided by the law that would be applied by the initially chosen forum. The facts in this problem would not meet this "inadequate remedy" standard. Thus, answer B is incorrect and assuming the court finds the chosen forum to be manifestly and significantly inconvenient, it will grant the motion in light of the availability of this alternative, more convenient forum. Answer C is incorrect because this fact, standing alone, is not a sufficient basis for invoking the doctrine of *forum non conveniens*. Answer D is also incorrect because this is not a sufficient basis for refusing to invoke the doctrine of *forum non conveniens*.

90. Issue: *Forum non conveniens*

The correct answer is **B**. The defendant here is relying on the doctrine of *forum non conveniens* as the basis for dismissing an action over which the court clearly has subject matter jurisdiction, in which venue lies, and with respect to a defendant over which it clearly has personal jurisdiction. Courts will grant this motion upon a showing not only that the chosen forum is extremely inconvenient but that a distinctly more convenient forum exists in which the court would have subject matter jurisdiction, venue, and personal jurisdiction. In the seminal case of *Piper Aircraft v. Reyno*, the Supreme Court indicated that, in determining whether an alternative forum exists, if the remedy provided by the alternative forum is so clearly inadequate or unsatisfactory that it is no remedy at all, the unfavorable change in law may be given substantial weight and the district court may conclude that dismissal would not be in the interests of justice. But the Court also stated that this standard is not met merely when the remedy provided by the alternate forum is either more difficult to obtain or not as lavish as that provided by the law that would be applied by the initially chosen forum. On the other hand, in this problem, the plaintiff would be completely divested of a right of action under Saudi law and this would result in no remedy at all. Consequently, the court would deny the motion to dismiss on *forum non conveniens* ground because even if the chosen Texas forum is manifestly and grossly inconvenient, under these circumstances, dismissal is not in the interests of justice. Thus, answer A is incorrect. Answer C is incorrect because this fact, standing alone, is not a sufficient basis for invoking the doctrine of *forum non conveniens*. Answer D is also incorrect because this is not a sufficient basis for refusing to invoke the doctrine of *forum non conveniens*.

91. Issue: Claim preclusion

The correct answer is **D**. In order to invoke claim preclusion, the proponent of that doctrine must satisfy three requirements: (1) that the two suits in question involve the same parties (or their privies); (2) that the two suits contained the same cause of action; and (3) there was a valid judgment on the merits in the first decided case. Since the first case was dismissed on jurisdictional grounds, there was no adjudication on the merits and so the final requirement for claim preclusion (res judicata) was not met. The fact that the other two requirements were met is not enough and so answers A and C are incorrect. Answer D is incorrect because this fact is irrelevant to the issue raised in this problem.

92. Issue: Claim preclusion

The correct answer is **C**. Although the states do not take a uniform position on this issue, a majority take the position that the expiration of the statute of limitations operates only to bar the remedy, i.e., to preclude the plaintiff from reasserting that claim in *that* jurisdiction. But as they do not find that the limitations period operates to extinguish the substantive cause of action, the dismissal is not deemed to preclude the filing of that same cause of action in a different jurisdiction with a longer (and unexpired) limitations period. (A minority of states adopt the view that the expiration of the statute of limitations does extinguish the substantive right and, therefore, a claim dismissed on that ground enjoys claim preclusive effect in other jurisdictions.) Therefore, under the majority view, answers A and B are incorrect because while they are factually true, the final requirement for invoking claim preclusion (res judicata) is not present. Answer D is incorrect because this factor is irrelevant to this question.

93. Issue: Issue preclusion

The correct answer is **C**. This problem raises the question of the application of the doctrine of issue preclusion (collateral estoppel). This doctrine is invoked to preclude the relitigation of an issue that has already been decided in a prior case involving a different cause of action than is involved in the subsequent proceeding. The consequence of invoking issue preclusion is merely to preclude relitigation of that issue. This is different than the consequence of invoking claim preclusion because when that doctrine is invoked, it results in the dismissal of the entire cause of action. The specific issue in this problem is whether the fact that the standard of proof governing the resolution of the same issue in the two proceedings is different means that the issue in the two cases is not the "same." In the criminal proceeding, the government had to establish that Melvin had stolen the money by a "beyond a reasonable doubt" standard, whereas it need only meet the lesser "preponderance of the evidence" standard in the subsequent civil action. Thus, as the Supreme Court held in *One Lot Emerald Cut Stones*, since this change in the standard of proof means that it is possible that the same evidence would result in a finding against the defendant in the second action, issue preclusion does not apply in this situation. Thus, the fact that the issue is the same is not dispositive and so answer B is incorrect. Answer A is incorrect because the parties to these two cases are identical. Answer D is incorrect because this fact leads to the conclusion that issue preclusion cannot be invoked.

94. Issue: Issue preclusion

The correct answer is **B**. This problem raises the question of the application of the doctrine of issue preclusion (collateral estoppel). This doctrine is invoked to preclude the relitigation of an issue that has already been decided in a prior case involving a different cause of action than is involved in the subsequent proceeding. The consequence of invoking issue preclusion is merely to preclude relitigation of that issue. This is different than the consequence of invoking claim preclusion because when that doctrine is invoked, it results in the dismissal of the entire cause of action. The specific issue in this problem is whether the fact that the standard of proof governing the resolution of the same issue in the two proceedings is different means that the issue in the two cases is not the "same." In the criminal proceeding, the government had to establish that Melvin had stolen the money by a "beyond a reasonable doubt" standard, whereas it need only meet the lesser "preponderance of the evidence" standard in the subsequent civil action. Since the government obtained a conviction in the criminal case, Melvin would be precluded from relitigating the issue of stealing the money in the subsequent civil action since the government had sustained the more rigorous standard of proof in the criminal case. Answer A is incorrect because the parties to these two cases are identical. The fact that the issue is the same is not dispositive as it is only one of the requirements for invoking issue preclusion and so answer D is incorrect. Answer C is incorrect because this fact leads to the conclusion that issue preclusion can be invoked.

95. Issue: Joinder of claims

The correct answer is **B**. Here we have a plaintiff asserting two claims against one defendant. The relevant standard is contained Rule 18 of the Federal Rules of Civil Procedure. Under Rule 18, a party can join as many claims as he or she has against that adverse party, regardless of whether the claims are related or unrelated. So the fact that the two claims here are unrelated is irrelevant to the question of their joinability. Therefore, answer A is incorrect. And since the question asked only if the claims were joinable, and not whether they fall within the court's subject matter jurisdiction, answers C and D are incorrect because this question is limited to joinability. While the court also would have to have subject matter jurisdiction over both of these claims, that issue is not raised in this problem.

96. Issue: Joinder of parties

The correct answer is **C**. This is a joinder of parties, and not a joinder of issues, problem. Costen is seeking to bring claims against more than one defendant in this suit, which automatically makes this a joinder of parties problem. The rule governing joinder of parties in federal court is Fed. R. Civ. P. 20. Under Rule 20(a)(2), a plaintiff can assert claims against more than one defendant as long as both of two requirements are met. First, these claims must arise out of the same transaction, occurrence, or series of transactions or occurrences. Second, the claims against both of the defendants must contain at least one common question of law or fact. Here the claims against both Lasso and Shelly arise out of the latter's alleged acts of harassment. So the first requirement of Rule 20 is met. Second, both of these claims require resolution of, among other things, the factual question of what Shelly did to Costen. Consequently, both requirements of Rule 20(a)(2) have been met. Unlike joinder of claims under Rule 18, joinder of parties under Rule 20 is not unlimited and, therefore, answer A is incorrect. Since the question raised in this problem is only joinability and not whether the court has subject matter jurisdiction, answers B and D are incorrect.

97. Issue: Joinder of counterclaims

The correct answer is **A**. Lasso's claim against Costen is a counterclaim and the rules governing joinder of counterclaims in federal court are found in Fed. R. Civ. P. 13(a) and (b). Rule 13(a) defines a compulsory counterclaim and 13(b) defines permissive counterclaims. Whether or not a joinable counterclaim is deemed to be compulsory is determined by assessing whether that counterclaim meets the requirements of 13(a) or (b). But that is not the issue here. The issue here is not whether the defendant was obliged to assert this counterclaim but whether he is permitted to do so, i.e., whether the counterclaim is joinable. The combination of these two subsections of

Rule 13 clearly means that all counterclaims are joinable. Like the text of Rule 18 with respect to joinability of multiple claims by one party against an opposing party, this Rule provides for unlimited right of joinder, regardless of whether the counterclaim is transactionally related to the claims in the plaintiff's complaint. Thus, answer D is incorrect. Whether or not the court has subject matter jurisdiction is another matter, but that is not being tested in this question. Consequently, answers B and C are incorrect.

98. Issue: Joinder of third-party claims

The correct answer is **C**. Shelly has filed a third-party complaint against Worldwide and this complaint contains two causes of action. The rule governing third-party complaints in federal court is Rule 14. Under Rule 14(a), third-party claims are joinable, but ONLY if they are for indemnity or contribution. Thus, unlike Rule 18 as to multiple claims by one party against one opposing party and Rule 13 as to counterclaims, the rule of joinder of third-party claims is limited. So the indemnity claim is joinable under Rule 14(a). And while it is true that the other non-indemnity claim is not joinable under Rule 14(a), it is joinable under Rule 18, which permits unlimited joinder of additional claims to a joinable claim or third-party claim. Thus, A is incorrect as it does not take account of the joinability of the second claim under Rule 18. Answer B is incorrect because both claims are joinable; the first under Rule 14(a) and the second under Rule 18. Answer D is incorrect because the indemnity claim is joinable under Rule 14(a).

99. Issue: Joinder of cross-claims

The correct answer is **D**. Lasso has filed a cross-claim against Shelly. The rule governing the joinder of cross-claims in federal court is Fed. R. Civ. P. 13(g). Like the rule regarding joinability of third-party claims, and unlike the rules governing the joinability of counterclaims, the rule governing joinability of cross-claims is limited. Rule 13(g) only permits the joinability of cross-claims that arise out of the transaction or occurrence that gave rise to the plaintiff's claims or to a counterclaim. Thus, answer B is incorrect. Lasso's cross-claim against Shelly for indemnity in connection with any liability it may incur as a result of Costen's claim against it clearly arises out of the occurrences that gave rise to the plaintiff's claim against Costen. This problem only asked whether or not the claim was joinable and not whether the court had subject matter jurisdiction over the claim. Therefore, answers A and C are incorrect.

100. Issue: Claim preclusion

The correct answer is **A**. The defendant asserted an affirmative defense to the plaintiff's breach of contract claim and then used that same theory offensively as the basis for a claim in the second lawsuit. An essential element of claim preclusion is that a plaintiff cannot "split" one single, indivisible cause of action into two parts. Claim preclusion precludes relitigation of any part of a cause of action that was the subject of a final adjudication on the merits, regardless of whether or not that particular portion of the claim was adjudicated in the first case. This same theory applies to what is called defense preclusion. Where, as here, a defendant asserts a theory as an affirmative defense in one case and then reasserts it against that same opposing party in a second case as the plaintiff seeking affirmative relief, this is called defense preclusion. In effect, the courts will not allow a defendant to split up the same issue into an affirmative defense in one case and a complaint seeking affirmative relief in the second case. What this requires the defendant to do in the first case is to both assert the defense and the claim for relief as a counterclaim. Thus, answer B is incorrect. Answers C and D are incorrect because those facts go to subject matter jurisdiction, which is not in issue in this problem.

101. Issue: Aggregation of value of diversity claims

The correct answer is **D**. This plaintiff has asserted a federal question (copyright) claim that falls under the court's §1331 subject matter jurisdiction. And the second claim by the plaintiff against this defendant is a diverse state law claim since the plaintiff is a citizen of Georgia and, per §1332(c), the corporate defendant is a citizen of Delaware (the state of its incorporation) and New York (the state of its principal place of business). But this claim seeks damages only in the amount of $60,000, which does not independently meet the amount in controversy requirement of §1332. But under the aggregation rules, a single plaintiff can aggregate the value of multiple claims against a single defendant. Thus, when combined with the value of the first claim (the fact that it is a federal question claim is irrelevant for aggregation purposes), the value exceeds the jurisdictional minimum. Thus, answer A is incorrect because original jurisdiction exists for this second claim under §1332. Answer B is incorrect because this is irrelevant to whether the court also can exercise original jurisdiction over the diverse state law claim. Answer C is incorrect because there is no attempt here to remove the case and §1441 is the removal statute.

102. Issue: Complete diversity requirement

The correct answer is **C**. The plaintiff asserted a federal question and a diversity claim against defendant Ace as well as this state law claim against Jackson, another diverse defendant. Consequently, the requirement in §1332 of complete diversity has been satisfied here. Plus, the $105,000 claim against Jackson satisfies the amount in controversy requirement and so original jurisdiction exists over this claim under §1332. Since there is original jurisdiction over this claim, there is no need to investigate the availability of supplemental jurisdiction under §1367 and so answer A is incorrect. Answer B is incorrect because this is not a removed case and §1441 is the removal statute. Answer D is incorrect because the fact that the two defendants are not diverse from each other is irrelevant to determining whether or not complete diversity exists with respect to this claim. As to it, the adverse parties are diverse.

103. Issue: Supplemental jurisdiction

The correct answer is **A**. Ace and Jackson are both citizens of New York and so they are not diverse. And this is a state law claim for indemnity. So there is no original jurisdiction over this claim. So we must examine whether the court can exercise supplemental jurisdiction over this claim. Since the lawsuit includes Emily's federal question claim against Ace, this is not a civil action of which the court has original jurisdiction founded solely upon §1332. Thus, the applicable provision is §1367(a) and not §1367(b). So answer B is incorrect. Under §1367(a), the court can exercise supplemental jurisdiction over this indemnity claim if it is part of the same constitutional "case" as any claim that falls within the court's original jurisdiction. The indemnity claim, by definition, arises out of the same nucleus of operative fact that gave rise to the copyright infringement claim. Thus, the court should exercise supplemental jurisdiction over this claim under §1367(a). There are no facts offered to suggest that the court will decline to exercise its discretion to use supplemental jurisdiction based on the factors set forth in §1367(c). Answer C is incorrect because §1367(b) is inapposite to this problem. Answer D is incorrect because the lack of diversity does not prevent the claim from falling within the court's supplemental jurisdiction.

104. Issue: Joinder of crossclaim

The correct answer is **B**. This is a cross-claim for indemnity. The Rule governing joinder of cross-claims is 13(g). Unlike Rule 18 and Rule 13 governing joinder of multiple claims by a single plaintiff against a single defendant and joinder of counterclaims, respectively, Rule 13(g) does not provide an unlimited right of joinder. It only permits joinder of cross-claims that are transactionally related to the original complaint or counterclaim. Thus, answer C is incorrect. And this indemnity claim, by definition, is transactionally related to the plaintiff's copyright claim against Ace. Answer A is incorrect because it is irrelevant to joinability; citizenship diversity goes to subject matter jurisdiction and not to joinability. Answer D is incorrect because these facts go to the issue of personal jurisdiction and not to joinability.

105. Issue: Joinder of claims

The correct answer is **A**. The plaintiff is seeking to join two claims against one defendant. Under Rule 18, there is no limit to the number of claims a party can join against another party as long as one of the claims is joinable. Answer B is incorrect because the nature of the claim is irrelevant under Rule 18. Answer C is incorrect because these facts go to subject matter jurisdiction and not to joinder. Answer D is incorrect because this fact goes to personal jurisdiction and not to joinder.

106. Issue: Supplemental jurisdiction

The correct answer is **C**. The adverse parties to this claim are both citizens of New York and so there is no original jurisdiction since the claim does not arise out of federal law. Since there is a federal question claim in the case, we turn to §1367(a) to determine whether or not the court can exercise supplemental jurisdiction over this claim. The requirement here is that this claim be part of the same "case" as claims within the court's original jurisdiction. This claim for withheld salary does not arise from the nucleus of fact associated with any other claim in the case. Consequently, the court cannot exercise supplemental jurisdiction. Answer A is incorrect because the lack of diversity is not always fatal to subject matter jurisdiction if the claim can fall within the court's supplemental jurisdiction. Answer B is incorrect because although Ace is a citizen of Delaware, it also is a citizen of New York per the definition of corporate citizenship in §1332(c). Thus, it is nondiverse from Jackson. Answer D is incorrect because this is irrelevant to the question of subject matter jurisdiction.

107. Issue: Joinability of counterclaims

The correct answer is **A**. Although this is a claim between co-defendants, it is not a cross-claim but a counterclaim to Ace's cross-claim against Jackson. Consequently, the correct Rule governing joinability is Rule 13(a) and (b) and not Rule 13(g). There is no limit on joinability of counterclaims and so this claim is joinable. Since it is not a cross-claim, there is no need to meet the Rule 13(g) requirement of transactional relatedness and so answer B is incorrect. Answer C is incorrect because this fact is irrelevant. Answer D is incorrect because the issue here is joinability, not subject matter jurisdiction.

108. Issue: Joinability of third-party complaints

The correct answer is **D**. This is a third-party claim. Accordingly, joinability is determined by Rule 14(a), which only permits joinder of third-party claims for indemnity or contribution. Since this claim is not an indemnity or contribution claim, it is not joinable. Therefore, answer C is incorrect because this is not an indemnity claim. Answer A is incorrect because it is irrelevant. Answer B is incorrect because this issue goes to subject matter jurisdiction and not to joinability.

109. Issue: Supplemental jurisdiction

The correct answer is **D**. The parties are both citizens of New York and this is a state law claim so there is no original jurisdiction over this claim. There is a federal question claim in the case so the question is whether this claim falls within the court's supplemental jurisdiction under §1367(a), which turns on whether this claim forms part of the same "case" as claims within the court's original jurisdiction. Because this claim alleges that Sue negligently maintained her property, it does not arise out of the nucleus of operative fact giving rise to any other claim in the case. So the court cannot exercise supplemental jurisdiction over it. Answer A is incorrect because the parties are not diverse and so the amount in controversy is irrelevant. Moreover, if the parties had been diverse, the amount in controversy requirement might have been met since Jackson is seeking both damages and an injunction and the court would have to place a value on the rights sought to be protected by the injunction, which could bump the amount in controversy above the minimum requirement. Answer B is incorrect because it is irrelevant. Answer C is incorrect because the fact that neither of the parties is a forum citizen might be relevant to personal jurisdiction, but is not relevant to subject matter jurisdiction.

110. Issue: Joinder of parties

The correct answer is **C**. Since Emily filed claims against two defendants, this raises the issue of joinder of parties defendant. Under Rule 20(a) multiple defendants can be joined if the claim against them arises out of the same transaction and there is at least one question of either law or fact common to the claim against all joined defendants. Both of these requirements are met here as both claims arise out of the decision not to publish Emily's book and involve the common question of why the book was not published, among others. Answer A is incorrect because this is irrelevant to joinder. Answers B and D are incorrect because they both relate to subject matter jurisdiction and not to joinder.

111. Issue: Supplemental jurisdiction

The correct answer is **C**. Karen and Ace are diverse but since the amount in controversy is only $75,000, it does not exceed $75,000 and therefore does not meet the amount in controversy requirement of §1332. Since this is a state law claim, the court does not have original jurisdiction over this cross-claim. Since original jurisdiction over the civil action is founded solely on §1332, whether or not the court can exercise supplemental jurisdiction over Karen's claim involves the application of §1367(b). This section prohibits the exercise of supplemental jurisdiction in diversity-based cases, but only over claims by "plaintiffs." Although Karen is a cross-plaintiff, this does not meet the §1367(b) requirement of being a plaintiff. She is a defendant and cross-plaintiff and so the limitation of §1367(b) is inapplicable here. So we must go to §1367(a) and ask if this claim forms part of the same "case" as claims over which the court has original jurisdiction. And it does, since this claim arises out of the accident that gave rise to the plaintiff's claims. So the common nucleus of operative fact standard of §1367(a) is met. Answer A is incorrect because the amount in controversy requirement has not been met so the fact of diversity is not sufficient to create original jurisdiction under §1332. Answer B is incorrect because while not meeting the amount in controversy requirement is a problem for original jurisdiction, it does not preclude the exercise of supplemental jurisdiction under §1367(a). Answer D is incorrect because, while true, it does not preclude the exercise of supplemental jurisdiction since the limitation in §1367(b) does not apply here because this was not a claim by a plaintiff.

112. Issue: Supplemental jurisdiction

The correct answer is **C**. This is a state law counterclaim between diverse parties but as to which the amount in controversy requirement has not been met. So there is no original jurisdiction over this claim. But since original jurisdiction over the civil action is founded solely on §1332, whether or not the court can exercise supplemental jurisdiction over Ace's counterclaim involves the application of §1367(b). This section prohibits the exercise of supplemental jurisdiction in diversity-based cases, but only over claims by "plaintiffs." Although Ace is a counter-plaintiff, this does not meet the §1367(b) requirement of being a plaintiff. Ace is a defendant and counter-plaintiff and so the limitation of §1367(b) is inapplicable here. So we must go to §1367(a) and ask if this claim forms part of the same "case" as claims over which the court has original jurisdiction. And it does, since this claim arises out of the accident that gave rise to the plaintiff's claims. So the common nucleus of operative fact standard of §1367(a) is met. Answer A is incorrect because the amount in controversy requirement has not been met so the fact of diversity is not sufficient to create original jurisdiction under §1332. Answer B is incorrect because while not meeting the amount in controversy requirement is a problem for original jurisdiction, it does not preclude the exercise of supplemental jurisdiction under §1367(a). Answer D is incorrect because, while true, it does not preclude the exercise of supplemental jurisdiction since the limitation in §1367(b) does not apply to this claim by a non-plaintiff.

113. Issue: Supplemental jurisdiction

The correct answer here is **C**. This is a state law claim between nondiverse parties so there is no original jurisdiction over this claim. It is a third-party claim in a case where original jurisdiction was founded solely on diversity. Thus, we need to look to §1367(b) but the ban on supplemental jurisdiction in §1367(b) only applies to claims by plaintiffs and this is a third-party claim by a defendant and so the limitation of §1367(b) is inapplicable. We then turn to §1367(a), which would allow supplemental jurisdiction if this claim forms part of the same case as the claims within the court's original jurisdiction. Since this third-party claim is for indemnity for any loss suffered by Ace in connection with the plaintiff's claim against it, the common nucleus of operative fact standard of §1367(a) has been met and therefore the court can exercise supplemental jurisdiction. Answer A is incorrect because the lack of diversity is not fatal to the exercise of subject matter jurisdiction. Answer B is incorrect because it is irrelevant. Answer D is incorrect because while this fact is true, the prohibition on supplemental jurisdiction contained in §1367(b) does not apply to this claim because it is not a claim by a plaintiff.

114. Issue: Venue

The correct answer is **D**. Since original jurisdiction was founded solely on diversity in this civil action, the relevant venue provision is §1391(a). Under §1391(a)(2), venue will lie in the district where a substantial part of the events that gave rise to the claim occurred. Since the accident occurred in the chosen venue, venue lies there. Answer A is incorrect because that fact goes to subject matter jurisdiction and not to venue. Answer B is incorrect because the residence of the plaintiff is irrelevant to the venue calculation required by §1391(a). Answer C is incorrect because although it is true, venue will still lie where the underlying events occurred pursuant to §1391(a)(2).

115. Issue: Venue

The correct answer is **C**. The venue statute only defines where a civil action may be brought and this has been construed to mean that the venue requirements do not apply to third-party claims. Thus, there is no need to consider venue over this third-party claim, which means that answer A is incorrect. Answer B is incorrect because this fact is relevant to subject matter jurisdiction and irrelevant to venue. Answer D is incorrect because that fact is relevant to subject matter jurisdiction and not to venue.

SKIP
7 & 8
& 10
& 20